Social Impact Investment

BUILDING THE EVIDENCE BASE

OECD

BETTER POLICIES FOR BETTER LIVES

Please cite this publication as:
OECD (2015), *Social Impact Investment: Building the Evidence Base*, OECD Publishing, Paris.
http://dx.doi.org/10.1787/9789264233430-en

ISBN 978-92-64-22893-1 (print)
ISBN 978-92-64-23343-0 (PDF)

Photo credits: Cover © Zurijeta /Shutterstock.com

Corrigenda to OECD publications may be found on line at: *www.oecd.org/about/publishing/corrigenda.htm.*

Foreword

New and innovative approaches are needed for addressing social and economic challenges. Social impact investment seeks to leverage innovation and apply measurement rigor to achieve social outcomes. This approach has become increasingly relevant in today's economic setting as social challenges have mounted while public funds in many countries are under pressure. Interest in social impact investment has grown considerably across several OECD countries including the G7 and G20. The field of social impact investment is expanding rapidly with a growing number of players entering the market. At the same time, greater knowledge about social impact investment as well as evidence about market activity and outcomes achieved to date are needed. The OECD social impact investment initiative is therefore timely as it aims to inform OECD member countries as well as non-OECD economies about developments in this area and the potential role of policy.

This report provides a framework for assessing the social impact investment market and focuses on the need to build the evidence base. The report highlights the importance of further international collaborations in developing global standards on definitions, data collection, impact measurement and evaluation of policies. In a fast evolving new area, experience sharing between players in the market is also vital. International organisations, such as the OECD can play an important role in facilitating these collaborations as well as conducting further analysis and data collection.

The project has been managed by Karen Wilson, consultant in the Structural Policy Division of the Directorate for Science, Technology and Innovation at the OECD. The report was written by Karen Wilson, Filipe Silva, Junior Policy Analyst in the Structural Policy Division of the Directorate for Science, Technology and Innovation and Dominic Richardson, Policy Analyst, Directorate for Employment, Labour and Social Affairs.

Social impact investment has become a growing area of interest within the OECD, linking to two strategic OECD initiatives, New Approaches to Economic Challenges (NAEC) and Inclusive Growth as well as ongoing work across a number of Directorates.

The OECD Committee for Industry, Innovation and Entrepreneurship (CIIE) agreed to the declassification of this report in January 2015.

ACKNOWLEDGEMENTS

The OECD is grateful to the Department of Employment and Social Development in Canada, the UK Cabinet Office, and the Bertelsmann Foundation for their support of this work.

In addition, the OECD would like to thank the Social Impact Investment Taskforce, established by the G8 during the UK Presidency, for their input throughout the process. A particular acknowledgement is extended to the Chair of the Taskforce, Sir Ronald Cohen, for his leadership, vision and drive in catalysing a global movement to build the social impact investment market.

The authors would like to thank the many experts who contributed to this work including all of the members of the Social Impact Investment Taskforce, their colleagues and others serving on the Working Groups and National Advisory Boards.

During the course of the project, the OECD held two Social Impact Investment Expert Group meetings and would like to thank all of those experts for their time and input. The full list of attendees is available in Annex A.

The authors would also like to thank Dirk Pilat, Deputy Director of the Directorate for Science, Technology and Innovation and Nick Johnstone, Head of the Structural Policy Division in the Directorate for Science, Technology and Innovation for their support of this work and input during the process and on drafts of the report.

In addition, the authors thank the Directorate for Employment, Labour and Social Affairs for their contributions to this work, particularly in Chapter 5 which uses data from the OECD Social Expenditure database and builds upon their work on social policy.

The authors also thank colleagues from other OECD Directorates for their input including the Centre for Entrepreneurship and the Development Centre's Network of Foundations Working for Development. Other Directorates engaged in the work have included Development Co-operation Directorate, Statistics Directorate, Directorate for Financial and Enterprise Affairs, and Directorate for Public Governance and Territorial Development.

Table of contents

Tables

Figures

Abbreviations

CBA	Cost-Benefit Analysis
CEA	Cost-Effectiveness Analysis
CIC	Community Interest Company
CSR	Corporate Social Responsibility
DFIs	Development Finance Institution
EVCA	European Venture Capital Association
EVPA	European Venture Philanthropy Network
GIIN	Global Impact Investing Network
LCC	Limited Liability Company
MRI	Mission-Related Investing
NAB	National Advisory Board
NPI	Non-Profit Institution
NSO	National Statistical Office
NVCA	National Venture Capital Association
PRIs	Program Related Investments
SE	Social Enterprise
SIFI	Social Investment Finance Intermediary
SII	Social Impact Investment
SIITF	Social Impact Investment Taskforce established under the United Kingdom's presidency of the G8
SPO	Social Purpose Organisation
SRI	Socially Responsible Investing
WGAA	Working Group on Asset Allocation
WGIM	Working Group on Impact Measurement
WGMA	Working Group on Mission Alignment

Executive summary

Social impact investment is the provision of finance to organisations addressing social needs with the explicit expectation of a measurable social, as well as financial, return. Social impact investment seeks to leverage innovation and apply measurement rigor to achieve social outcomes. This approach has become increasingly relevant in today's economic setting as social challenges have mounted while public funds in many countries are under pressure. New approaches are needed for addressing social and economic challenges, including new models of public and private partnership which can fund, deliver and scale innovative solutions from the ground up.

Social impact investment has evolved over the past decade as the result of a number of factors, including a growing interest by individual and institutional investors in tackling social issues at the local, national or global level. The recent economic crisis has further highlighted the tremendous social and economic challenges facing countries across the globe. Governments are seeking more effective ways to address these growing challenges and recognising that private sector models can provide new innovative approaches. Private sector investors, such as foundations, high net worth individuals and institutional investors are increasingly interested in making investments that can have both a social and a financial impact. Chapter 2 provides further background on the evolution of the market as well as highlights parallels to traditional capital markets.

Awareness of the potential opportunities of social impact investment has grown considerably across several OECD countries and non-OECD economies including in the G7 and G20. In the context of the United Kingdom's G8 presidency in 2013, the UK Prime Minister hosted a G8 Social Impact Investment Forum in London in June 2013 and launched the Social Impact Investment Taskforce. As one of the outcomes of the G8 Social Impact Investment Forum, the OECD was asked to produce a report on the social impact investment market. This report seeks to provide a basis for building the evidence base of the evolving social impact investment field. It follows an overview paper on social impact investment, published by the OECD in July 2014.[1]

A growing range of actors are emerging in the social impact investment market to form an ecosystem consisting of social ventures, intermediaries and investors committed to addressing social needs. Government also plays a key role in the ecosystem, in terms of setting conditions for the enabling (or hindering) environment as well as potential indirect or direct engagement in the market. Framework conditions (e.g. tax and regulation) have a significant impact on the social impact investment market. Chapter 3 provides a framework for looking at the various components of the social impact investment ecosystem and the different channels through which social impact investment takes place. The ecosystem framework outlined in the paper highlights the importance of starting with the social needs and beneficiaries, not with the financial instruments being applied. In many cases, a mix of financing instruments need to be used and tailored in a way that best meets the needs of the social delivery organisation and, more importantly, the end beneficiaries.

The social impact investment market is in the early stages of development. The international initiative, led by the Social Impact Investment Taskforce, established under the United Kingdom's presidency of the G8, has helped in raising awareness and clarifying the broader definition of social impact investment. However, for purposes of scoping and sizing the market, it is essential to work towards a precise common understanding of what is meant by social impact investment. This is important for policy makers, researchers and practitioners as well as for the overall development of the market.

Chapter 4 of this report expands on existing definitions with the aim of spelling out the underlying criteria for assessing a social impact investment. It also provides a framework to help in working towards a common detailed definition, which in turn will facilitate data collection and a better understanding of the market. Seven key characteristics of social impact investment are identified in the paper including the social target areas, the beneficiary context, the nature of good/service provided (public/private), delivery organisation social intent, measurability of social impact, investor social intent and return expectations. Within each characteristic, a further set of related attributes are highlighted and possible boundaries are suggested to help further the discussion about what should and should not be considered social impact investment.

The market is evolving in various ways across OECD countries. This is influenced by the differences in the country context including history, social needs and value systems. In addition, the ways in which social and financial systems are structured will determine the role and mix of public and private capital and therefore the potential role of social impact investment. The variation in these contexts can provide indications in terms of which social impact investment approaches may be more appropriate in some sectors than in others, and easier to implement in some countries than in others.

Social needs have been increasing in many countries requiring both more efficient and more effective social service delivery. Trends in public expenditure show that services are taking up more of the social protection budget, in some cases exceeding cash spending. However, social service delivery is complex and entails a number of specificities and potential challenges for social delivery organisations as well as for social impact investment models. The extent to which any investment can make a social impact will rely on the type and extent of need – and demand for improvement – across an array of social outcomes. Social outcomes evolve in different directions, in different social sectors, for different reasons. These topics are discussed in detail in Chapter 5.

A stronger evidence base is critical to increasing engagement in the social impact investment market and facilitating the development of a global market. Different players involved in the market, including policymakers, have been calling for a better and more accurate understanding of the size, scope, evolution and potential of the market. However, the specific data requirements for each of these players can differ. It is therefore important to clarify these needs and agree on a set of target indicators before embarking on a data collection exercise, especially given the challenges in collecting social impact investment data.

Currently, available data on social impact investment is very limited. Various approaches have been used to collect data and estimate the scope of the social impact investment market, but each of these approaches requires strong assumptions or has other limitations. Being able to collect comprehensive transaction data in an efficient manner would help in building a better understanding of market activity. This would require specific common definitions of social impact investment as well as harmonisation of data collection efforts to ensure comparability across countries and regions. Various efforts are underway but the best way forward will likely involve a partnership between key players involved in data collection across countries. Current data sources and data collection processes are outlined in Chapter 6.

The public sector can play a catalytic role in the social impact investment market in terms of creating a conducive regulatory environment, encouraging greater transparency and taking concrete steps to help develop the market. Policy actions in some countries have addressed regulatory issues, notably in terms of setting up legal structures to accommodate social impact investment market actors. Several policy interventions have sought to enhance supply of social impact investment. Some governments have provided support through tax credits (and tax-advantaged funds), guarantees or subsidies, established and co-invested in social impact investment funds. Other governments have focused on developing the social impact investment market infrastructure through the creation of intermediaries such as specialised wholesale banks, exchanges (or trading platforms) and other channels to facilitate the links between supply and demand for social impact investment (investors and delivery organisations). Additionally some have sought to stimulate demand by providing support to delivery organisations/investees through technical assistance or by encouraging procurement.

Depending on the type of actions taken, they might be implemented at the international, national or local level. However, actions initiated in one country or region may not be appropriate for another – policy objectives, experience and local context must be taken into account. In particular, differences in the context of developed and developing countries should be considered when applying social impact investment models. Social impact investment can catalyse additional capital flows into developing economies, critical to the high-level dialogue on Financing for Development and the implementation of the new universal Sustainable Development Goals.

When or if policies with the objective of supporting social impact investment, such as tax incentives, are put in place, it is important that the policy interventions are well targeted, transparent and well-coordinated with existing policies as well as with the market. Policies should also be consistent over time so that market players both understand the implications of the policies and have some visibility in terms of how long the policies might be in place. Evaluation of the policies is also important to make sure that they are having the intended results. Chapter 7 highlights some of the social impact investment policies currently in place in the G7 countries and Australia and discusses broader policy implications in building the market.

Social impact investment can potentially provide new ways to more efficiently and effectively allocate public and private capital to address social and economic challenges at the global, national and local levels. It provides a vehicle for bringing innovative into existing delivery systems for addressing social issues and also provides incentives for more rigorous measurement of outcomes. While these innovative new approaches will not replace the core role of the public sector or the need for philanthropy, they can provide models for leveraging existing capital using market-based approaches with potential to have greater impact. However, given that social impact investment is a nascent field, concrete evidence is needed in terms of its impact to date. In particular, further work is needed to demonstrate the gains from the social impact investment approach compared to existing social service delivery models.

This report provides a framework and approaches for thinking about definitions and data in the social impact investment market, highlighting the implications for policy. The paper seeks to deepen the discussions about the definitions of social impact investment to enable clearer comparisons within and across countries as a step towards building the necessary market evidence base. The report highlights the importance of further international collaborations in developing global standards on definitions, data collection, impact measurement and evaluation of policies as well as experience sharing between players in the market. International organisations, such as the OECD can play an important role in facilitating these collaborations as well as conducting further analysis and data collection.

In particular, further work is needed to assess the role of SII in an expanded set of countries, including developing countries. Further OECD work will expand the scope to the G20 countries and beyond. Changes in the development finance landscape will require new measures to capture the full spectrum of financing sources and financial instruments. The shift in sources of financial flows will also require further analysis of the trade-offs in terms of various types of financing, including SII, as well as a scoping in terms of which market settings are more appropriate for various types of financing.

There also needs to be deeper knowledge sharing about social impact investment practices. Currently there is a lot of show casing but not enough learning about what is working and what is not, including about the true costs, efficiencies and outcomes of particular practices. More detailed case studies which outline the roles of various actors and the processes involved in structuring social impact investment products would be useful along with more formal evaluations of these practices.

Social impact investment touches many different fields of analysis. To minimise the challenges of building a robust evidence base for the whole SII market, detailed analysis could initially focus on certain cases and/or social need areas. This more focused approach is important as there are bound to be variations in appropriate policies within and across sectors. As part of the next phase of the work on social impact investment, the OECD could, for example, focus on a particular area and work on building the evidence base across difference countries and cases.

Given the growing level of activity in the social impact investment market around the world, it is crucial to build the evidence base to understand what works and ensure that capital is put to work on interventions that achieve the intended impact. This includes systematically collecting data and being able to use the data in a cross-country comparable way to better track the development of the market.

NOTE

1. Wilson, K. E. (2014), "New Investment Approaches for Addressing Social and Economic Challenges", OECD Science, Technology and Industry Policy Papers, No. 15, OECD Publishing, http://dx.doi.org/10.1787/5jz2bz8g00jj-en.

Chapter 1

Overview of social impact investment

This chapter provides an overview of social impact investment highlighting its policy relevance in today's economic and social environment. It starts by discussing the growing need for new approaches for solving economic and social challenges and the role that social impact investment can play in that respect. It then provides an overview of current trends, opportunities and challenges in the social impact investment market. It also shows how the market is evolving and compares that to parallels in the evolution of the capital markets.

1.1. The need for new approaches to address social and economic challenges

Social impact investment (SII) is the provision of finance to organisations with the explicit expectation of a measurable social, as well as financial, return. Social impact investment has become increasingly relevant in today's economic setting as social challenges have mounted while public funds in many countries are under pressure. New approaches are needed for addressing social and economic challenges, including new models of public and private partnership which can fund, deliver and scale innovative solutions from the ground up.

SII involves private investment that contributes to the public benefit. Investors can range from those who are willing to provide funding for organisations that are not able to generate market returns to more traditional investors but with an interest in also having a social impact.

Figure 1.1. **A spectrum of capital**

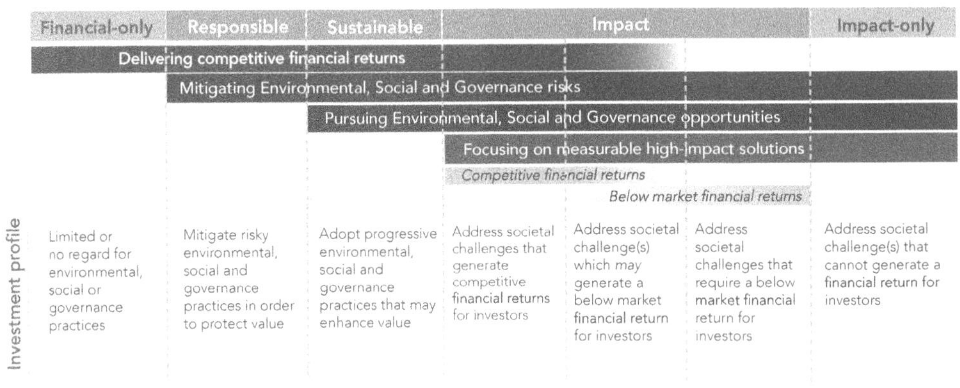

Source: SIITF WGAA (2014).

A growing number of high net worth individuals, family offices, foundations and institutional investors have become interested in finding investments that deliver both a social and a financial return. Financial goals can range from capital preservation to a market rate of return. Social goals can include improving socio-economic, social or environmental conditions.

Social impact investment has evolved over the past decade as the result of a number of factors, including a growing interest by individual and institutional investors in tackling social issues at the local, national or global level. The recent economic crisis has further highlighted the tremendous social and economic challenges facing countries across the globe. Governments are seeking more effective ways to address these growing challenges and recognising that private sector models can provide new innovative approaches.

The growth of social enterprises over the past several decades (Noya, 2009; OECD/EU 2013) has also contributed to the emergence of social impact investment. Social enterprises seek to develop innovative ways to tackle social challenges. These organisations need capital to grow but often face greater obstacles than mainstream firms (Noya, 2009). In response, a social impact investment market has grown over the past decade to address these needs as well as to develop additional approaches for financing solutions to social issues.

Increasingly, experts suggest that social or environmental factors can impact a company's bottom line and therefore are important factors in business, markets and competition (Porter and Kramer, 2011). The traditional view has been that pursuing social or environmental objectives could require some financial trade-off, although not necessarily a financial loss. As experience in the market has developed, a growing number of examples demonstrated that, in certain areas, social impact investments can generate both a financial and social return. It is in these areas that social impact investors can play a role in providing private capital to address social challenges in innovative news ways.

The market is evolving in various ways across OECD countries. This is influenced by the differences in the country context including history, socials needs and value systems. In addition, the ways in which social and financial systems are structured will determine the role and mix of public and private capital and therefore the potential role of social impact investment.

1.1.1. Motivation for the OECD report

In the context of the United Kingdom's G8 presidency in 2013, the UK Prime Minister hosted a G8 Social Impact Investment Forum in London in June 2013 (HM Government, 2013c). The Forum was attended by ministers and other policy, business and civil society leaders from across the G8 countries and provided an opportunity to launch processes and initiatives to facilitate the development of the market on a global scale. A Social Impact Investment Taskforce (SIITF) was established, consisting of one public and one private sector representative from each of the G7 countries and the European Union.[1] The taskforce includes an observer from Australia and one from OPIC as a representative of Development Finance Institutions.

As one of the outcomes of the G8 Social Impact Investment Forum,[2] the OECD was asked to produce a report on the Social Impact Investment market. The work on the OECD report took place in parallel with the work of the Social Impact Investment Taskforce and its four Working Groups.

National Advisory Boards, created in late 2013 in the G7 countries and Australia, met on a regular basis to provide input to the work of the Taskforce as well as to identify ways to develop the social impact investment market in each country. Reports from the Taskforce, its Working Groups and its National Advisory Boards were published in September 2014.[3] These reports were developed to feed into future international policy discussions, with G8 and G20 countries and beyond.

This report is the result of the first phase of the OECD work in the context of this international initiative. The paper seeks to provide a framework for building the evidence base of the evolving social impact investment market. This report, which was supported by several G8 countries, builds upon existing work at the OECD including the research on social impact investment and new investment approaches conducted with support from the Bertelsmann Foundation during 2013 (Wilson, 2014) as well as other work across the OECD.

As an integral part of this process, the OECD worked together with SII data experts and academics to identify major data gaps and challenges, as well as to discuss ideas for better data collection in the future. The OECD organised two SII Expert Meetings in the first half of 2014. The first meeting took place on 21 March 2014 at the OECD headquarters in Paris. The second meeting was held on 18 June 2014 at the UK Cabinet Office, London. The OECD thanks the UK Cabinet Office for hosting the meeting as well as all participants in both workshops for their input into the process. The list of participants in both workshops can be found in Annex A.

Social impact investment has become a growing area of interest within the OECD, linking to two strategic OECD initiatives, New Approaches to Economic Challenges (NAEC) and Inclusive Growth as well as ongoing work across a number of Directorates. This includes ongoing work within the Directorate for Science, Technology and Innovation on entrepreneurship financing and innovation, including inclusive innovation. It also builds upon work conducted in the Directorate for Employment, Labour and Social Affairs related to social policy. In addition, the project links to work conducted over the past decade in the Centre for Entrepreneurship's LEED programme on social enterprise, the Development Centre's Network of Foundations Working for Development and their recent work on venture philanthropy and the Development Cooperation Directorate's initiative on public/private financing for development. There are also further connections to ongoing work by the OECD Secretariat in the Statistics Directorate, Directorate for Financial and Enterprise Affairs, the Directorate for Public Governance and Territorial Development, and other OECD Directorates.

1.2. Evolution and trends in the social impact investment market

Social impact investment began to emerge about a decade ago, although there was significant activity prior to that (Saltuk et al, 2013). However, socially-conscious investing is not a new phenomenon and has origins dating back several centuries.

A number of decades ago, Socially Responsible Investing (SRI), a practice in which investors screen out companies with perceived negative products or practices, began to interest investors (Bridges Ventures, 2012). This later led to a broader and growing group of "responsible" investors seeking socially responsible and sustainable investments (Addis et al, 2013). Today, a growing number of companies have begun focusing on environmental and social issues or practicing corporate social responsibility (CSR). However, as noted by the SIITF, these investments have "tended to focus on the intentions and approaches of companies rather than on the measured achievement of impact goals" as required by social impact investors (see Chapter 3 for further details on definitions of SII).

Figure 1.2 below, developed by the Social Impact Investment Taskforce, shows the impact continuum in which social impact investment lies in between "sustainability" (specifically referring to CSR, ESG and SRI) and philanthropy but does not include either – only investments (e.g. not grants) that proactively seek a measurable social impact alongside a financial return. However, many providers of grants, such as foundations, are also social impact investors. Also, some businesses that have traditionally practiced CSR, ESG or SRI have also moved into the social impact investment space. The role of foundations and other investors is discussed further in Chapter 2.

Social impact investors seek market-based solutions to the world's most pressing challenges, including sustainable agriculture, affordable housing, affordable and accessible healthcare, clean technology, and financial services for the poor (GIIN, 2014). Chapter 4 discusses the areas that fall within the OECD SII definition.

Social impact investments can be made across geographies, sectors, and asset classes and can have a wide range of return expectations. Often these investments are made with multiple types of investors providing different forms of capital. By combining various forms of capital with different return requirements, social challenges can be addressed in more scalable ways than possible by government alone (Rangan et al, 2011).

Initiatives being led by governments, foundations, investors and others have helped accelerate the market in the past few years (Jackson and Associates, 2012). A number of OECD countries, such as the United Kingdom, the United States, France and Australia, have played a leading role in developing the social impact investment market. There have also been significant developments and experiments in the past several years in many other developed and developing countries which are contributing to the development of new models and approaches.

Figure 1.2. **The SIITF impact continuum**

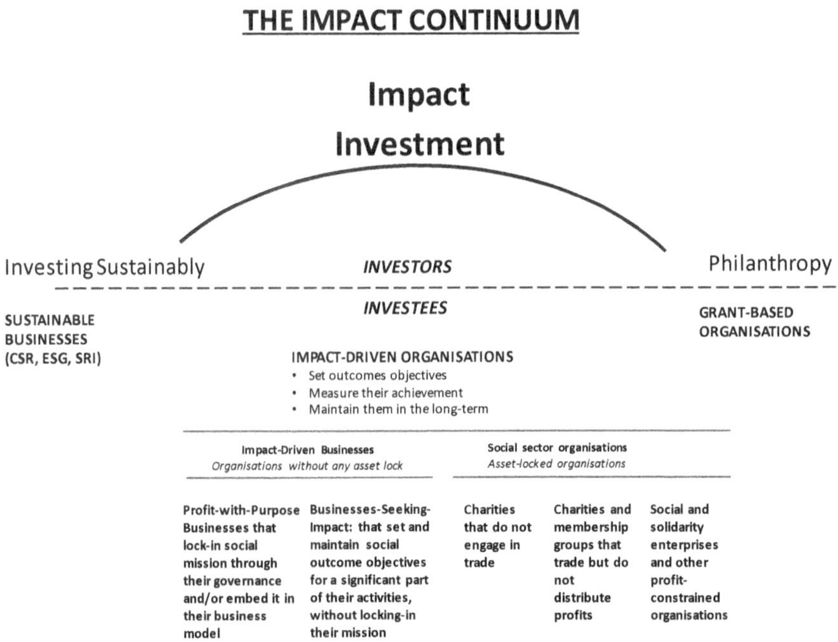

Source: SIITF (2014).

Given that countries are at different stages of development, the experience sharing process of the Social Impact Investment Taskforce established by the G8, and the associated National Advisory Boards in the G7 and Australia, has been helpful in raising awareness about social impact investment and how countries might engage. These activities have also helped spur additional action within those and other countries and attract new players to the market.

While Phase I of the international initiative focused on the social impact investment markets and policies in G7 countries and Australia, there was a Taskforce Working Group looking into the implications for international development[4].The next phase of the initiative is planned to expand its engagement and focus to the G20 countries and beyond. There is a growing recognition that traditional sources of development financing, in particular official development assistance (ODA), are not sufficient to address the scale and complexity of today's global development challenges. Partnerships are needed that encourage better collaboration between the public and private sectors and ways need to be found to use ODA in a smart way to facilitate these partnerships as well as mobilise additional resources.

International aid agencies are searching for new tools, including results-based financing, outcomes-based approaches, market-based solutions and different forms of public-private partnerships, to increase their effectiveness and long-term development impact while working with the limitations of tighter budgets. Social Impact investing has the potential to catalyse new capital flows into developing economies, translating experiences, policies and approaches from developed countries into the emerging and less developed country context.

While the social impact investment market has been growing significantly and has drawn increasing interest and attention, it is still in the early stages of development (Kohler et al, 2011) and is only a small share of the global capital markets today (Saltuk et al, 2014). While difficult to measure for a variety of reasons including the lack of clear definitions and the diversity of sectors and approaches across geographies, the social impact investment market potential has been estimated to be significant. This is due to growing interest among foundations and mainstream investors as well as an intergenerational transfer of wealth, estimated at USD 41 trillion that is expected to take place over the next 50 years with nearly USD 6 trillion of that expected to be directed towards social issues (Rangan et al, 2011).

Figure 1.3. **Microfinance: Clients and institutions globally, 1997-2011**

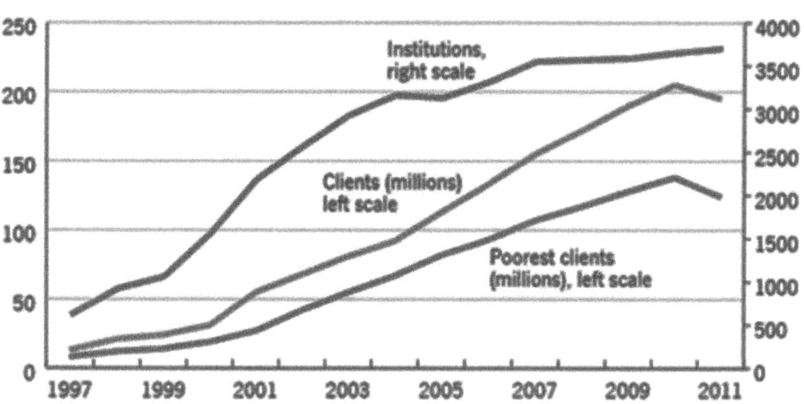

Source: OECD based on Maes and Reed (2012).

The microfinance industry was an early model of changing approaches to financing which also addressed social needs. The microfinance market is estimated to include over USD 50 billion of loans given to over 100 million micro-entrepreneurs, mostly in developing countries (Rangan et al, 2011). From 1997-2007, microfinance grew at a rate of 38% per year in terms of the number of clients although growth has slowed in more recent years (Addis et al, 2013). The Monitor Institute and J.P. Morgan estimated similar possible annual growth rates for the social impact investing market (Freireich and Fulton, 2009; O'Donohoe et al., 2010).

It should be noted, however, that the microfinance industry had a lot of government support, in the form of grants and low-interest loans, before it got to the more stable and self-sustaining commercial state that it has now reached.

1.3. Parallels to the evolution of capital markets

Social impact investment financing models are emerging at multiple levels and in parallel to traditional markets. As in capital markets, financial intermediation plays a critical role as there are information asymmetries between investors and investees. Intermediaries play a critical role in connecting demand and supply, particularly in financial markets that are less developed.

Figure 1.4. **Financial intermediation**

In the traditional capital markets, intermediation is focused on financial dimensions. The social impact investment market is more complex as social dimensions also need to be valued. Transaction costs in social impact investment are high due to fragmented demand and supply and the complexity of deal structuring. For these reasons, coordinating capital for social ventures is more difficult than in the venture capital industry (Kohler et al., 2011). Given the high costs and early stage of market development, there is a lack of brokers, advisors, exchanges and other market mechanisms, resulting in a market with imperfect market competition.

The degree of financial sector development within a country can potentially have an influence on the development of the social impact investment. Figure 1.5 below shows the difference in financial sector development in the G7 countries and Australia according to a 2012 World Economic Forum report. It can be noted that the most active social impact investment markets are currently in the two countries with the most developed financial sectors.

Figure 1.5. **Financial sector development**

Scores 1 to 7, as of 2012

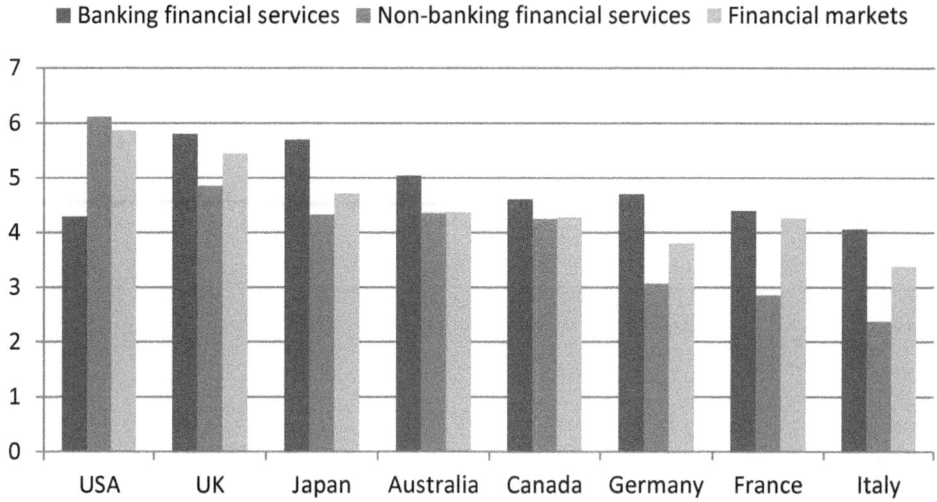

Source: OECD based on WEF (2012).

The development of capital markets often leads to availability of a range of products across the risk return spectrum. Different types of financing instruments may be more appropriate for different stages of the development of a venture (Wilson and Silva, 2013). Figure 1.6 illustrates a typical life-cycle of a firm along with the various stages of financing and types of financing instruments. The figure below highlights the complexity of financing and the need for a mix of instruments to address the various growth phases of a firm.

As in the mainstream financial markets, investment evolution is not necessarily linear, although it is often assumed to follow a path from individual transactions, to boutique offerings to funds, funds of funds and ultimately fully "liquid", or tradable, capital markets where investors have a range of choices to buy and sell investments (Bugg-Levine and Emerson, 2011).

While the players, financing needs and mix of instruments differ from traditional finance, social impact investment instruments span asset classes and can include equity, quasi-equity, loans and bonds. A growing range of social impact investment instruments have been developed, all with a different financial/social return profile. However, given the early stage of market development, there is a lack of products across the risk/return spectrum making it more difficult to attract investors, particularly more mainstream ones.

Figure 1.6. **Life-cycle of a firm and stages of financing**

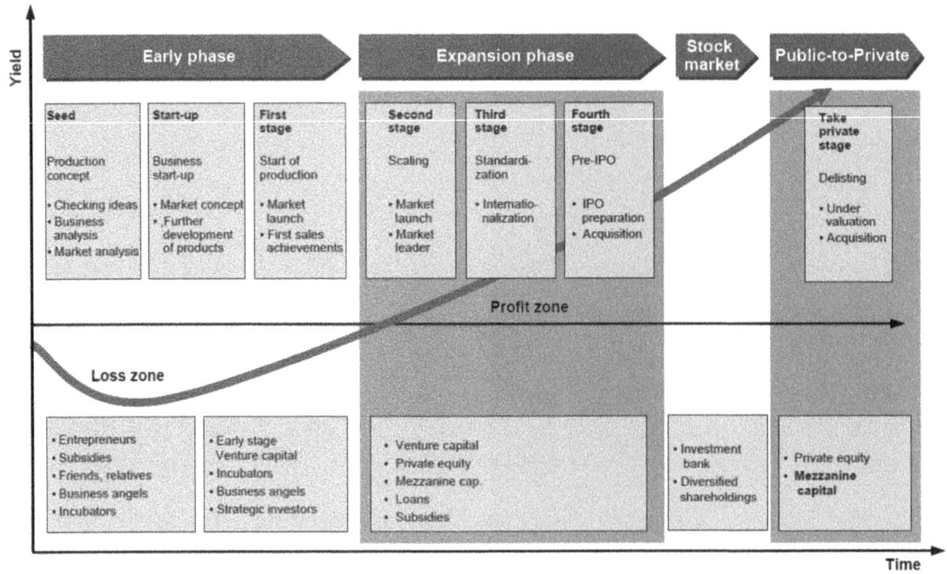

Source: OECD (2013a) based on Natusch (2003).

The existence of vibrant entrepreneurial finance markets can facilitate the development of the social impact investment market as experience with financial market tools can help in building the SII market. In fact, many people in SII were active in investment banking, private equity, venture capital and/or angel investing.

Comparisons are sometimes made between the evolution of the social impact investment market and the venture capital industry (Cohen and Sahlman, 2013). The venture capital industry, which was first created in 1946, grew over several decades through a series of US government interventions, including a legislation in the 1950s that allowed privately funded investment firms to provide capital to early-stage funds, ERISA in 1978 which enabled pension funds to invest in venture capital firms and a lowering of the capital gains tax rate (Freireich and Fulton, 2009). In the 1970's, the industry began growing in Europe and later in other parts of the world. Pioneers in the venture capital industry included Sir Ronald Cohen, one of the leaders and key drivers of the social impact investment movement, in the United Kingdom and globally, and the Chairman of the Social Impact Investment Taskforce established by the G8 in 2013.

Notes

1. In mid-2013, Russia had chosen not to participate as the topic was not a priority for Russia.

2. Further information available at: https://www.gov.uk/government/groups/social-impact-investment-taskforce.

3. The Taskforce, NAB and Working Group reports are available at: www.socialimpactinvestment.org/.

4. See the Working Group report for further details: Social Impact Investment Taskforce (2014), Subject Paper of the International Development Working Group: International Development.

References

Addis, R., J. McLeod, and A. Raine (2013), "IMPACT Australia: Investment for Social and Economic Benefit", Australian Government, Department of Education, Employment and Workplace Relations, November.

Bridges Ventures (2012), "Sustainable & Impact Investment - How we define the market", London, August.

Bugg-Levine, A and J. Emerson, (2011), "Impact Investing: Transforming how we make money while making a difference", Wiley: Jossey-Bass, September.

Cohen, Sir R. and W.A. Sahlman (2013) "Social Impact Investing Will Be the New Venture Capital", HBR Blog Network, 17 January, http://blogs.hbr.org/2013/01/social-impact-investing-will-b/.

O'Donohoe, N., C. Leijonhufvud and Y. Saltuk (2010), "Impact Investments: An Emerging Asset Class", J.P. Morgan Securities plc, GIIN and Rockefeller Foundation, November.

Freireich, J. and K. Fulton (2009), "Investing for Social and Environmental Impact: A Design for Catalyzing an Emerging Industry", Monitor Institute, January.

GIIN (2014), Global Impact Investing Network website. Available at: www.thegiin.org/cgi-bin/iowa/resources/about/index.html, accessed 3 February 2014

HM Government, United Kingdom (2013c), "G8 Social Impact Investment Forum: Outputs and Agreed Actions", UK Cabinet Office, London, July.

Jackson, E.T. & Associates (2012), "Accelerating Impact: Achievements, Challenges and What's Next in the Impact Investing Industry", The Rockefeller Foundation, July.

Kohler, J., T. Kreiner, and J. Sawhney (2011), "Coordinating Impact Capital: A New Approach to Investing in Small and Growing Businesses: An examination of impact investors and phased investing for the launch and growth of social enterprises", Santa Clara University and

The Aspen Network of Development Entrepreneurs (ANDE), Santa Clara, California, July.

Maes and Reed, *State of the Microcredit Summit Campaign Report*, Microcredit Summit Campaign, 2012.

Natusch, Ingo (2003), "Mezzanine Method of Financing", Round Table Talks, IKB – Deutsche Industriebank, October; Document available at: www.brsi.de/pdfs/Mezzanine_Finanzierungsformen_engl.pdf.

Noya, A. (ed.) (2009), *The Changing Boundaries of Social Enterprises*, Local Economic and Employment Development (LEED), OECD Publishing, http://dx.doi.org/10.1787/9789264055513-en.

OECD (2013a), "Alternative Financing Instruments for SMEs and Entrepreneurs: the Case of Mezzanine Finance", internal working document, Centre for Entrepreneurship, SMEs and Local Development.

OECD/EU (2013) Policy brief on social entrepreneurship, Luxembourg Publications Office of the European Commission

Porter, M and M. Kramer (2011), "Creating Shared Value: How to reinvent capitalism and unleash a wave of innovation and growth", Harvard Business Review, January – February.

Rangan, K.V., S. Appleby, and L. Moon (2011), "The Promise of Impact Investing", Harvard Business School, Background Note No. 512-045, Boston.

Saltuk, Y, A. Bouri, A. Mudaliar and M. Pease (2013), "Perspectives on Progress: The Impact Investor Survey", Global Social Finance, J.P. Morgan and the Global Impact Investing Network, London, January 7.

Saltuk, Y., A. Idrissi, A. Bouri, A. Mudaliar, and H. Schiff (2014), "Spotlight on the Market: The Impact Investor Survey", Global Social Finance, J.P. Morgan and the Global Impact Investing Network, London, 2 May.

SIITF (2014), "Impact Investment: The Invisible Heart of the Markets", Social Impact Investment Taskforce, London, September.

WEF (2012), "World Economic Forum Financial Development Report 2012", World Economic Forum, Geneva.

WGAA (2014), "Allocating for Impact", Working Group on Asset Allocation (WGAA), Social Impact Investment Taskforce established by the G8, September.

Wilson, K. E. (2014), "New Investment Approaches for Addressing Social and Economic Challenges", *OECD Science, Technology and Industry Policy Papers*, No. 15, OECD Publishing, http://dx.doi.org/10.1787/5jz2bz8g00jj-en.

Wilson, K. and Silva, F. (2013), Policies for Seed and Early Finance: Findings from the 2012 OECD Financing Questionnaire, OECD Science, Technology and Industry Policy Papers, No. 9, OECD Publishing.

Chapter 2

The Social impact investment framework

This chapter provides a framework for looking at the social impact investment market, starting with social needs and then looking at the demand and supply sides of the market as well as the role of intermediaries. Examples of key types of players in the market are given to provide further context. The role of the enabling environment is also discussed as a key part of the framework.

The statistical data for Israel are supplied by and under the responsibility of the relevant Israeli authorities. The use of such data by the OECD is without prejudice to the status of the Golan Heights, East Jerusalem and Israeli settlements in the West Bank under the terms of international law.

2.1. The social impact investment framework

A growing range of actors are emerging in the social impact investment market to form an ecosystem consisting of investors, social ventures and intermediaries and a comprehensive picture of the SII market requires assessing the different components of the market (Figure 2.1). The main components of the ecosystem are driven by SII demand (including social needs and social service providers), SII supply (i.e. pools of capital and investors) and the role of SII intermediation and intermediaries (including transactions and financing instruments). The enabling environment, including framework conditions (e.g. social systems, tax and regulation), also can play a critical role in the social impact investment market and must be taken into consideration when looking at the SII ecosystem.

Figure 2.1. **Social impact investment market framework**

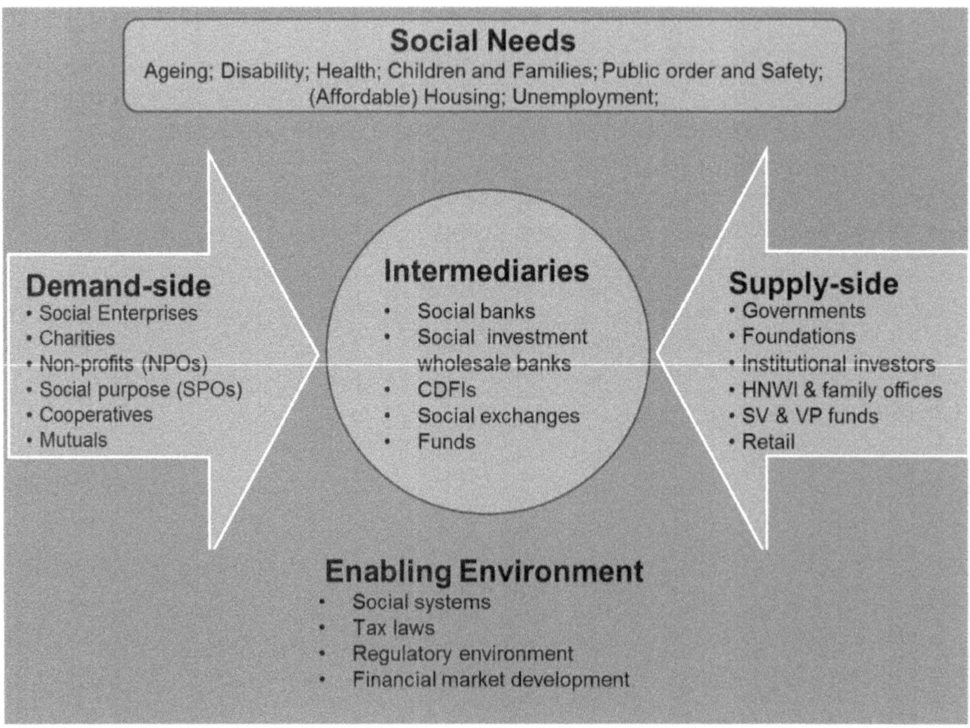

Source: OECD.

Progress in the social impact investment market will depend on different stakeholders working together to build critical mass by developing the market, tools and practice. Those stakeholders include investors, investees and intermediaries as well as policy makers, all with varying interests and motivations. Building trust is important, and market transparency is essential to building this trust (IIPC, 2014).

2.2. Social needs

Social impact investment starts with the social need being addressed. These can cover a wide range of social need areas such as ageing, disability, health, children and families, affordable housing, unemployment, etc. The types of beneficiaries of social impact investment can also vary. These issues are described in further detail in Chapter 3. In addition, the social context and social systems within a country can vary dramatically and have a huge impact on the potential opportunities for SII. This is discussed in detail in Chapter 4.

2.3. Demand side

The key drivers in addressing social needs are the service delivery organisations. These organisations can include community organisations, charities or non-profit organisations, social enterprises, social businesses, and social impact-driven businesses. In some countries, only non-profit organisations are considered "social", however rules are changing to include for-profits with a targeted social purpose.

Demand-side actors seek to find new models to deliver social impact and create new markets through their social ventures (HM Government 2012). The term "social enterprise" began gaining visibility in the 1990s (OECD, 2000) as an innovative business model for meeting social and economic objectives, that embodies constraints on the distribution of profits and/or assets, however, the organisational structures and legal forms vary widely across countries (Noya, 2009).

Social delivery organisations operate in a wide range of geographies and sectors and therefore have varying financing needs. The development of financial instruments across the full risk/return spectrum is needed to meet the varying needs of these enterprises. However, this requires a better understanding of which financial instrument and funding model would be most effective for social ventures at various stages of development (Evenett and Richter, 2013). In addition, some of these organisations are becoming hybrids (Glänzel et al., 2013) and therefore are pursuing a mix of funding approaches. The OECD CFE/LEED has worked extensively on social enterprises, particularly at the local level (e.g. OECD, 2013b).

Box 2.1. **Financing challenges for social enterprises**

Access to capital is vital to the creation and development of social enterprises. Social enterprises are usually financed by a combination of market resources (e.g. the sale of goods and services), non-market resources (e.g. government subsidies and private donations or investments), and non-monetary resources (e.g. volunteer work).

Grant financing, whether from governments, foundations or others, may be required at an early stage of development and can be reduced as social enterprises build scale and market capacity. However, in some cases, secure long-term funds may be needed, for example, in certain sectors in which social enterprises are not able to become self-financing but whose activities provide public benefits and/or reduce public costs.

For social enterprises that are to obtain additional financing, a diversity of private market financial products that correspond with the life-cycle of social enterprises (from start up or even pre-start up, to consolidation and growth) is needed. One of the key financial products used by most mainstream enterprises is bank loans. However, in most OECD countries, social enterprises have difficulty obtaining access to credit. Traditional financial institutions generally refuse to lend to social enterprises because they do not meet their established client criteria and are not seen as offering sufficient guarantees. Consequently, they must seek new financial partners or reduce their development ambitions.

OECD countries are seeing the emergence of a number of new financial instruments and actors to support social enterprises, together with broader investment criteria for existing financial actors and behavioural shifts among actors already engaged in supporting civil society initiatives (Noya, 2009). Interest and activity in social impact investing, which focuses on proactive investment choices aimed at supporting social enterprises that can have a strong social impact while seeking some financial return, is growing and can contribute to the scaling and growth of social enterprises.

Source: OECD/EU (2013).

A recent survey showed that business model execution and management is seen by investors as the highest risk to their investments in social ventures (Saltuk et al, 2014). As with traditional businesses, some new ventures will fail to achieve their goals. The reasons for failure of these ventures can vary from management, strategy or funding to regulatory and administrative barriers. However, reports have shown that social enterprises do better and fail less than for-profits because they are built on real problems and (unfortunately) the market is there and growing.

Social impact investors, as well as targeted policies, can play a role in improving the effectiveness of social ventures (Jackson and Associates, 2012). Social impact investors can help social delivery organisations by providing not only financing but perhaps more importantly, support on strategy, management and growth (Bannick and Goldman, 2012). Helping social entrepreneurs grow their ventures to scale is the key to maximising impact (Koh et al., 2012). The success of social impact investment is reliant on the long term sustainability and performance, both social and financial, of the impact organisations, for-profit and not-for-profit, in which the investments are made (Bannik and Goldman, 2012).

Investment readiness remains a key issue for social ventures in many countries. Enhancing the investment readiness and business capability of these organisations is important to enable them to access SII (HM Government, 2011). Creating more investable social ventures will require improving financial skills in the social sector as well as developing a better understanding of risk and how to price it (Brown and Swersky, 2012).

The United Kingdom launched a GBP 10 million strategic fund, the Investment Contract and Readiness Fund, to help social enterprises secure capital. The Fund helps with investment readiness and enables social ventures to access new forms of investment and compete for public service contracts. Grants between GBP 50 000 and GBP 150 000 are available to social ventures which go on to raise at least GBP 500 000 investment, or which want to bid for contracts over GBP 1 million. The Boston Consulting Group (BCG) conducted an independent interim review by in April 2014 and determined that the fund was having a "significant and positive impact" (BCG, 2014).

Social ventures can also face challenges in a number of other areas including finding adequate legal forms or conforming to impact assessment standards. Transaction and reporting requirements can be high for social enterprises (OECD, 2013b). As the focus on impact measurement has increased, so have the pressures on social enterprises to comply with a varying set of standards, many of which can be time consuming and do not always feed back into the management and objective setting processes within the organisation. Efforts are being made to develop a streamlined set of reporting standards.

Mission drift is another challenge for social impact investors and entrepreneurs. This can be overcome, to some degree, by incorporating social parameters (clauses in term sheets and covenants) into investment documents to make sure both the investor and investee remain aligned to the social mission. A Working Group of the SIITF was dedicated to this important topic and it is also covered further in Chapter 4.

2.4. Supply side

On the supply side, capital providers are increasingly interested in social impact investment as a way to diversify their investments and pursue social, as well as financial, goals. These include foundations, high net worth individuals and philanthropists, banks and other financial services firms and intermediaries. To date, the most active social impact investors have been high net worth individuals (HNWI) and family offices, who have more flexibility and autonomy than other investors (WEF, 2013). Interested high net worth individuals may invest individually or possibly through the small but increasing number of angel investment groups focused on social impact investment (OECD, 2011).

Foundations have played a critical role in the development of the social impact investment market (Koh et al., 2012). This role can range from building market infrastructure, such as Rockefeller Foundation has done in the United States and the Bertelsmann Foundation in Germany, to providing "catalytic" capital or actively investing, through programme related investments (PRI) programmes. Private foundations have the advantage of being independent from government and the markets and therefore are in a position to take on greater risk than other private investors and provide long-term "patient" capital. This gives them the freedom to explore and create innovative ways to address social, economic and environmental challenges.

Grants, both public and private, continue to play an important role by providing "first loss" or "catalytic" funding (GIIN, 2013). Grants and technical assistance are often needed before or alongside SII to help social ventures addressing social challenges develop commercially-viable solutions (Bridges Ventures, 2012). In addition to foundations, Development Finance Institutions (DFIs) have also played an important role as "catalytic" funders in the market.

While grants are not considered social impact investment, foundations can and do engage in the market through market building activities as well as through mission-related or program-related investments (Rangan et al., 2011). However, in those cases, it is important for the foundations to distinguish between grants, which in reality provide a 100% "subsidy" versus investments which involve risk and therefore an expectation of returns. In essence, there are various forms of support and financing for social ventures and different types of investors will look at the spectrum of investment options with their own risk/return requirements in mind. Return expectations are discussed in further detail in Chapter 3.

Box 2.2. **PRI: Bill & Melinda Gates Foundation (United States)**

The Gates Foundation focuses on tackling poor health and extreme poverty globally, as well as education challenges in the United States. The Gates Foundation has been a very active and leading player in SII, in particular through a PRI approach that was adopted in 2009. Since then, funds through PRIs, to organisations tackling social issues have risen considerably reaching an allocation of more than USD 1.5 billion as of 2012. PRIs allow the foundation to work in close collaboration with the private sector to align the foundation's programmatic (social) goals with the financial objectives of other investors.

Table 2.1. below provides examples of investments that while having the potential to generate financial returns, are made within the scope of the programmatic and charitable objectives of the Gates Foundation. In particular, the Africa Health Fund tackles poor health and ASA International contributes to ending extreme poverty in Africa and Asia. The investments into Aspire Public Schools, a charter school management organisation in the United States, address educational challenges of low-income communities and students.

Table 2.1. **Examples of Gates Foundation PRI activity**

PRI Name	Social focus	Financing Instrument	Goal
Africa Health Fund	Tackling poor health	Private equity fund (co-investment)	Improve access to finance for African healthcare companies
ASA International	Financial services for the poor (microfinance)	Low interest loan	Affordable financial services to low-income individuals and small businesses in underserved markets in Africa and Asia
Aspire Public Schools	Education	Partial backstop guaranty (with co-guarantors)	Aspire opens and operates charter schools in low-income neighbourhoods

Source : Gates Foundation website, www.gatesfoundation.org/How-We-Work/Quick-Links/Program-Related-Investments/.

The PRI approach goes beyond grant-making models traditionally used by foundations insofar as it builds on a set of financial instruments ranging from direct debt, equity, guaranties and (debt or equity) funds. At the same time, PRIs are linked to the foundation's grant programme themes. These financing instruments are used to further the programmatic and charitable objectives of foundations. The use of innovative funding mechanisms allows foundations to attract other (co-) investors and involve them in the social mission. In doing so, PRI is a model aiming to tackle social challenges and yield social outcomes as its primary objective. In some cases PRIs have the potential to generate financial returns (usually below market), but this is never the main purpose of the investment. These investments count towards the foundation's charitable distribution requirement, but can be considered as assets (or liabilities) that leverage the foundation's endowment.

According to the recent J.P. Morgan and Global Impact Investing Network (GIIN) survey, program-related investments (PRI) allow foundations to use "more appropriate tools for achieving programmatic objectives in certain instances" and "access to additional vehicles through which impact can be delivered (e.g. investment funds)" (Saltuk et al, 2014). A growing number of foundations are engaging in PRI. Box 2.2 provides some examples from the Bill & Melinda Gates Foundation's approach to programme related investing.

Some pension funds, insurance companies and other institutional investors have also entered this market (Wood et al, 2012). However, these mainstream investors tend to focus on investments with at least a market risk adjusted financial return due to fiduciary responsibilities (WEF, 2013). At the same time, other private firms, such as investment banks, private banks and private equity funds are exploring areas in which they can provide capital to profitably grow businesses in various social sectors. A recent World Economic Forum report provides practical steps to be taken in order for mainstream investors to engage in social impact investment (WEF, 2014).

Despite the increased interest among institutional investors, securing commitment from traditional investors continues to be a challenge. The approach to institutional investors needs to be structured in way that works for them and in a language they can understand. Initiatives, such as GIIN, ANDE and SOCAP, which build links between mainstream and social impact investors, can help to create awareness and increase interest. Institutional investors also have certain legal requirements which can create barriers to social investing (Wood et al, 2012). These issues are discussed further in the recent SIITF Working Group paper "Allocating for Impact".

Another challenge in engaging mainstream investors is the lack of sufficient absorptive capacity for capital (Freireich and Fulton, 2009). There is a scarcity of high quality investment opportunities into which larger amounts of capital can be deployed. More products are being developed, across the risk return spectrum, into which institutional investors can deploy social impact investment funds.

Some social impact investors are finding it helpful to focus on investment within specific sectors (Bannick and Goldman, 2012). This enables a concentration on providing expertise and building the necessary links within a specific sector and thinking about social businesses in the context of the sector ecosystem.

Individual citizens are also able to participate, whether through investments in the local community or through pension funds with a social return element, such as the "Solidarity Funds" in France. Solidarity funds, or "90/10" funds as they are often called, are based on employee pension plans and savings. Companies with over 50 employees can contribute and 10% of those funds must be invested in government-recognised "solidarity organisations". These funds are regulated by Finansol and managed in partnership with banks, microfinance institutions and investment firms. Initially, only non-profit organisations could earn the "solidarity" label, but the rules have changed to now also include commercial businesses with a social mission. Solidarity finance provides a way to engage "retail" money in the social sector, however, the assumption is often made that the returns on that 10% will be low (or that returns on the other 90% will be higher).

According to a recent Triodos report, "retail" or citizen participation in social impact investing is a promising development which can be vital to the long term success of the market. The report suggests the creation of social impact investment funds for retail investors, the expansion of impact-enabled employee savings and pension plans with funds dedicated to social impact investment and tax incentives for retail impact investments (Triodos, 2014).

Crowdfunding platforms are also increasingly providing access for retail investors to support social enterprises. While most crowdfunding for social causes is donation-based (Wilson and Testoni, 2014), increasingly, equity crowdfunding platforms are providing investment opportunities in some countries, although equity crowdfunding is still not allowed in many countries due to investor protection rules.

Finally, the public sector clearly plays a central role through the commissioning of social services by national government departments, local authorities and other government agencies as well as through direct or indirect support of the SII market. These topics are discussed in further detail in Chapter 4.

2.5. Intermediaries

Intermediaries can play a pivotal role in developing the social impact investment ecosystem. They provide the links between investors, investees and others in the market and provide innovative new solutions to improving efficiencies in the market. They play functions such as creating liquidity in the market and facilitating payment mechanisms which can also help to lower costs and reduce risks in the market (WEF 2013). They also provide advice as well as help in structuring deals and in managing funds.

The lack of efficient intermediation in the social impact investment market translates into higher transaction costs caused by fragmented demand and supply as well as complex deal structuring (Freireich and Fulton, 2009). The early stage of ecosystem infrastructure development impedes the dialogue between investors and social ventures, which makes it difficult to break down historical barriers between philanthropy and investment (Freireich and Fulton, 2009). Platforms are needed to provide accessible distribution systems and offer comparable product performance (Jackson and Associates, 2012). This will also allow better matching of investor and investee risk/return profiles.

Intermediaries can include commercial banks, investment banks, independent financial advisors, brokers, dealers, and exchanges. The creation of new specialist intermediaries and the strengthening of existing ones are important for creating a well-functioning ecosystem as well as enabling deal flow (Jackson and Associates, 2012). Various types of intermediaries are needed to serve all sizes of impact-driven organisations (Addis et al, 2013) and players in the ecosystem need to be encouraged and incentivised to collaborate.

2.5.1. Social venture funds

Social venture funds started over a decade ago and are becoming more prevalent. However, most of the funds are young and small, often without a track record, making it difficult to attract institutional investors (GHK, 2013). These typically follow a venture capital type of model but can include a mix of instruments beyond equity. Like venture capital funds, social venture funds take a portfolio approach to investing to balance risks and returns (Saltuk, 2012).

The number of social investment funds is increasing. Some of these funds are independent while others are affiliated with large banks or development institutions. Funds might focus on certain sectors, geographies or investment stages. They typically target market returns, investing through a mix of grants, subsidised loans and equity investments. More recently, fund-of-funds have been created to provide greater scale and diversity for institutional investors (WEF, 2013).

Social investment fund managers often have a close hands-on relationship with the social purpose organisation they support, driving innovative and scalable models of social change (EVPA, 2011). Some may take board seats at these organisations, and most are more involved at the strategic and operational levels.

Models for these funds can vary. For example, Social Venture Fund (headquartered in Germany but expanding to other countries as well) invests in social enterprises, which have innovative and entrepreneurial driven solutions for urgent social and environmental challenges. Bridge Ventures, a private investment firm, created in the United Kingdom in 2002, is dedicated to using an impact-driven investment approach to create superior returns for both investors and society at-large. Bridges Ventures began by investing in for-profit ventures in underserved communities and later created a Social Entrepreneurs Fund.

Social venture investors face challenges in assessing the growing number of projects. It requires systems, structures and processes. Mission drift can be a danger. It is important for there to be in as much direct contact as possible between fund managers and the "front line" (i.e. to listen to people who are actually doing the work) to truly understand the operating model and key success factors.

2.5.2. Social stock exchanges

Over the past several years, social stock exchanges have been created in both OECD countries and non-OECD economies. These include Social Stock Exchange (SSE) in London, Nexii in South Africa, and Impact Investment Exchange (IIX) Asia in Singapore (the latter two have since merged). These exchanges target smaller high growth enterprises in sectors such as health, education, environment, social and affordable housing, sustainable forestry and organic agriculture and other "base of the pyramid" interventions. Social stock exchanges seek to build a platform for social businesses to attract capital from individuals, private clients, family offices, foundations and institutional investors who are seeking both a social and a financial return.

These markets facilitate the purchase of stocks and bonds in companies that have both economic and social returns. These could be either non-profit or for-profit companies. For-profit companies can either issue shares representing ownership in their companies or issue bonds. Not-for-profit companies can utilise the stock exchange to issue bonds. The London Social Stock Exchange was launched in 2013 with the aim to become a FSA-authorised and regulated investment exchange for trading in securities of social enterprises and other social purpose businesses (HM Government 2013a). Supported by the London Stock Exchange Group, the SSE has a number of listed member companies.

The London SSE seeks to connect socially focused businesses with investors looking to generate social or environmental change as well as financial return from their investment. This is done by providing investors with information to identify and compare organisations that deliver value to society and the environment. The London SSE seeks to have a transparent, independent and rigorous admission process to ensure that the companies listed adhere to a clear set of values, standards and disclosures.

In 2013, Nexii and IIX Asia agreed to collaborate to strengthen and standardise the impact investing sector and later merged. Impact Exchange aims at being a social stock exchange with significant global reach, from Africa to Asia, two regions in need of capital assistance for sustainable development. Impact Exchange aims at becoming a platform for the public to invest in and trade shares of social enterprises while assuring mission alignment to social and/or environmental impact.

Intermediaries/advisors pay an application fee as well as an annual membership fee, which allows them to become members of the exchange. The companies or organisations don't need to be profitable when they join as the rules allow a three year window to become profitable (but based on a clear plan to do so). They pay for advisors as well as for the application and listing fees. Rigorous reporting requirements are part of eligibility. Organisations can be delisted or suspended if they do not comply.

2.5.3. Building market infrastructure and capacity

Creating the necessary infrastructure and building capacity is important to the development of the market and, as a result, a number of these initiatives have been led by governments, foundations and others (IIPC, 2014). To build the market, collaboration is crucial for ensuring that the roles of the various players are complementary (HM Government, 2013c). Trust and open communication is important for the process of market building. This provides the basis for the creation of new innovative models, which can be tested in a continual process of development and growth of the market.

Box 2.3. **Big Society Capital (BSC)**

Big Society Capital (BSC) is an independent financial institution in the United Kingdom established to develop and shape a sustainable social impact investment market in which social sector organisations can access the capital they need to increase their positive impact on society. BSC was launched in April 2012 and is the first social impact investment bank in the world.

BSC is a "social impact investment wholesaler" which provides finance to social impact investment finance intermediaries (SIFIs). These are organisations that provide appropriate and affordable finance and support to frontline charities, social enterprises and voluntary organisations (the social sector). BSC seeks to achieve its objectives by addressing key market failures in the social impact investment market, ultimately increasing the social impact achieved by frontline social sector organisations.

The five key areas of activity include supporting or providing: capitalisation and balance sheet growth; risk and working capital; sustainability and organisational growth; market mechanisms and infrastructure; advice, skills and information.

BSC was funded from GBP 400 million in dormant bank accounts and with GBP 200 million from the four major banks (Barclays, HSBC, Lloyds, and Royal Bank of Scotland). Most of BSC's GBP 600 million in capital is for investment in social finance investment intermediaries. BSC seeks to achieve financial sustainability over the long term.

Source: www.bigsocietycapital.com.

In the United Kingdom, Big Society Capital (BSC) acts as a wholesale investor for social impact investment by investing in intermediaries and championing the sector to the public, stakeholders and investors (Box 2.3). BSC has also commissioned a number of research reports on the social impact investment market and created guides and standards for investors and social enterprises (Addis et al, 2013).

However, in most countries, intermediaries either do not exist or are not sufficiently developed to effectively facilitate the matching of SII demand and supply. Intermediaries and advisors are hard to finance due to high operating costs. Currently, most survive through donations. Others take transaction fees or a share of equity. Policy makers, foundations and others can play a role in the early stages of building the market but need to identify ways that the intermediaries can be sustainable in their own right over time.

Intermediaries, such as the Global Impact Investing Network (GIIN), described in Box 2.4, can also play an important role in encouraging "traditional" financial players to enter the market.

Box 2.4. **Global Impact Investing Network (GIIN)**

The Global Impact Investing Network (GIIN) is a nonprofit organisation dedicated to increasing the scale and effectiveness of impact investing. The GIIN was conceived in October 2007, when the Rockefeller Foundation gathered a small group of investors to discuss the needs of the emergent impact investing industry. In June 2008, a broader group of 40 investors from around the world met to discuss what it would take for the impact investing industry to be able to solve more social and environmental challenges with greater efficiency. Just over a year later, the GIIN was formally constituted as an independent organisation.

The GIIN addresses systemic barriers to effective impact investing by building critical infrastructure and developing activities, education, and research that attract more investment capital to poverty alleviation and environmental solutions. Specific initiatives include outreach, network membership, the Investors Council, ImpactBase (an online global directory of impact investment vehicles) and IRIS.

Impact Reporting and Investment Standards (IRIS) is a set of metrics that can be used to describe an organisation's social, environmental, and financial performance. IRIS is designed to address a major barrier to the growth of the impact investing industry - the lack of transparency, credibility, and consistency in how organisations and investors define, measure, and track their performance.

Source: www.thegiin.org.

For investors to enter the SII market, the measurement of social impact is critical. Rating and certification agencies therefore play an important role in the market (WEF, 2013). The IRIS initiative, mentioned in the Box 3.4, aims to encourage the adoption of a standard format for reporting for social, environmental, and financial performance. The Global Impact Investing Ratings System (GIIRS) is a ratings agency and analytics platform for impact investors. GIIRS reviews, evaluates and scores the social and environmental impact of companies and funds along a number of dimensions of social and environmental impact.

2.5.4. Social investment instruments

As referenced in Chapter 1, the social investment market is developing in parallel to the current investment market in terms of products, funds and market structures. Typically, social impact investment entails the use of debt or equity instruments to deliver a social or environment "return" as well as a financial return. The balance between the two will differ depending on where the instrument lies on the spectrum as well as how well the investors and investees perform (Kramer and Cooch, 2006). New products and structures are continuing to be developed to meet the growing needs in the market (HM Government, 2013a).

As in traditional finance, social investment instruments can include grants, loans, guarantees, quasi-equity, bonds and equity. However, more products, in the form of tailored financial instruments, are needed to match the various risk profiles and development stages of social ventures. Currently, there is a lack of a capital aggregation ladder (capital needed for social enterprises to grow and scale their business models) common to other asset classes.

While there are differences across countries, in general there is a shortage of risk capital available, at both the early stage as well as at the growth stages. The ecosystem needs to be able to take risks and have the capital to fund innovative ventures. In some countries there are still some legal complications for social equity investment but attempts are being made to solve it with quasi-equity and other instruments.

Today, most social investment is still in the form of grants, primarily from the philanthropic community, or secured loans. Venture philanthropists, who can operate across the spectrum of investment return, typically offer non-returnable grants for a purely social return while others use loan, mezzanine or quasi-equity finance for blended risk-adjusted financial and social returns (EVPA, 2011). Venture philanthropists provide substantial and sustained financial support to a limited number of organisations. Support typically lasts three to five years although it can also be longer with a goal of helping the organisation become financially self-sustaining by the end of the funding period (EVPA, 2011). Foundations have become increasingly interested in these models. A recent OECD publication highlights some foundation's experiences to date in developing countries (OECD, 2014).

There is a need for hybrid models using a combination of instruments. Increasingly, foundations are co-mingling traditional grants with social investment funds to combine their own experience and assets with those of commercial investors (HM Government, 2013a). Most deals require a mix of different types of instruments.

"Pay for Success" instruments such as Social Impact Bonds (SIBs), first launched in the United Kingdom a few years ago, are capturing attention within the industry as well as in the broader public as an innovative new way to finance solutions to social issues. These public-private partnership models can contribute to much needed innovation in financing models as well as improvement in public service delivery. However, they can also be complex and time consuming to structure and implement (Addis et al, 2013).

A SIB is a type of public-private partnership that embeds a pay-for-success scheme, commissioned by public authorities, foundation or corporations to provide social (goods and) services. SIB commissioners have clear priorities in terms of social goals that need to be achieved in a more efficient way. So, they set up predefined and measurable target social outcomes. As depicted in Figure 3.2 below, social service providers, with a track record in addressing that particular social need, are provided funding in the form of investment by private investors. The investors in the SIB are then repaid based on the achieved outcomes, defined *a priori* by the SIB commissioner.

It is important to note that the focus on measuring outcomes (e.g. reduction of infection rates) is different from a focus on measuring outputs (e.g. number of vaccines provided). Transparency is ensured as outcomes are evaluated by an independent entity. The investors will be repaid, in tranches over time, only if the agreed upon outcomes are achieved. The payments and any positive returns on investment should reflect the innovation and more efficient social service provision provided by the social service delivery organisation. For information on the evaluation of the first SIB created (in the United Kingdom), see Chapter 6.

The SIB model spread quickly across the United Kingdom and to other countries, including the United States and Australia. These SIBs focus on a range of social issues including, for example, criminal justice, child/family support, homelessness, employment, and health. These and many other new models are currently being developed in a growing number of countries. A list of SIBs is provided in Annex 2.1.

Figure 2.2. **The SIB model**

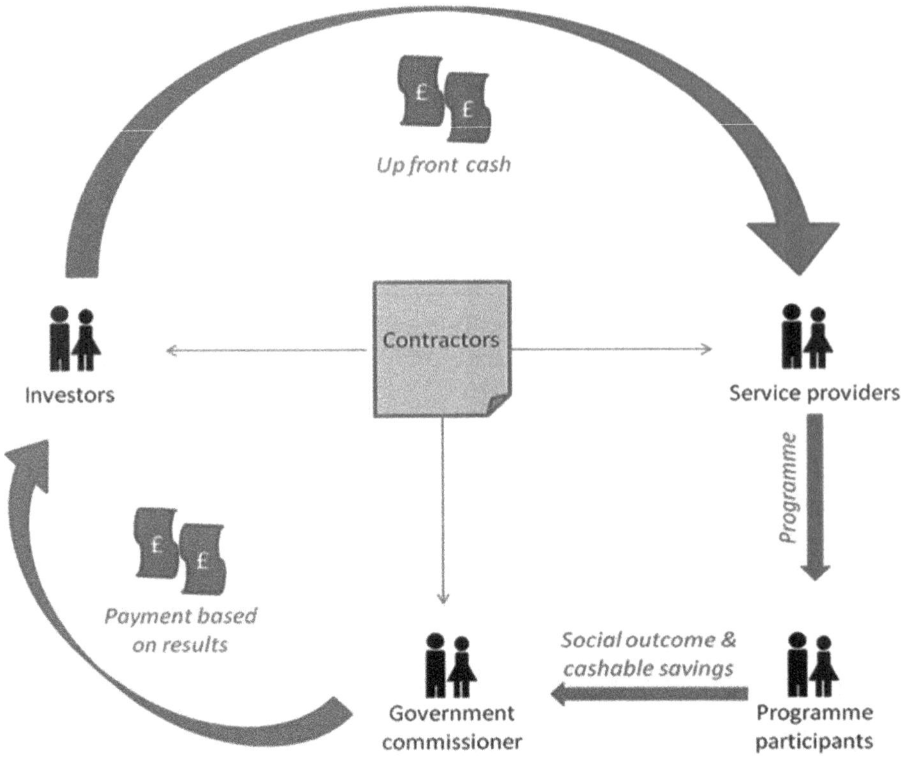

Source: UK Cabinet Office, available at: https://www.gov.uk/social-impact-bonds.

Building on the SIB model, Development Impact Bonds (DIB) are also structured as pay-for-success schemes but focused on developing countries. As with SIBs, investors are paid on the basis of whether the pre-defined social/development outcomes are achieved. DIBs seek to improve the effectiveness of traditional donor-funded projects by shifting the focus onto implementation quality and the delivery of successful results by introducing private sector actors who may be better-positioned than the public sector to take on risks associated with innovation. However, it should be noted that applying these models in developing countries might entail additional challenges such as the extent to which DIB contract terms can be enforced. Annex 2.1 includes a number of DIBs currently being developed in countries such as India, Mozambique or Uganda. Contrary to SIBs, the typical DIB commissioner is not local governmental authorities but rather international organisations or development agencies – e.g. the United Kingdom's Department for International Development recently announced a DIB to invest in the prevention of deadly sleeping sickness in Uganda.

2.6. Enabling environment

The general framework conditions in a country can have a significant impact on the development of financial markets in general and the social impact investment market in particular. The existence of vibrant entrepreneurial finance markets can facilitate the development of the social impact investment market as experience with financial market tools can help in building the SII market (in fact, many people in SII were active in investment banking, private equity, venture capital and/or angel investing).

The SII market is evolving in various ways across countries. This is influenced by the differences in the country context and, in particular, the ways in which social and financial systems are structured which determines the role and mix of public and private capital (Wilson, 2014). Chapter 4 provides further details on the social systems in the selected countries.

In addition, political economy considerations also play an important role, since SII may be perceived differently across and even within countries. Indicators that might proxy social perceptions can shed some light on these aspects. Information on social perspectives is usually obtained through surveys such as the World Values Survey or the European Social Survey Additional data may also be available from the OECD (e.g. Society at a Glance; Better Life Index, Annex 5.2), World Bank indicators or the Social Progress Index. Annex 5.1 provides a list of data sources with links to where this type of data can be found.

For the SII market to function well, the necessary legal frameworks and structures need to be in place for social ventures as well as streamlined regulations and requirements for investment (Thornley et al, 2011). This includes corporate structures more suitable to social ventures as existing structures (either for-profit or non-profit) may restrict the ability or flexibility of these organisations to attract investments in some countries. A number of new corporate structures are developing in various countries to meet the needs of hybrid social ventures. Hybrid corporate structures seek to blend for-profit and non-profit sources of funds to enable social organisations to pursue their mission (Rangan et al, 2011). Legal structures are discussed in further detail in Chapter 4 and also in Chapter 6.

Barriers to the development of the SII market include legal and civil frameworks for the creation and regulation of social organisations, as well as the availability of finance and market information for start-ups in this field. A number of countries have established legal precedents or civil codes for social ventures which aim to facilitate new social start-ups, reduce risks for both entrepreneurs and potential investors, as well as make up part of the system of regulation and review needed to assess social impact in countries.

Regulation, however, is a more complex contributor to the picture; on the one hand regulation may facilitate third party evaluation of social impacts (as with benefit corporations – see Reiser, 2013) and in turn help lower the risk for investors seeking social returns, and on the other may create additional costs for the enterprises themselves.

As discussed earlier, the availability of financial capital for social enterprises is a critical factor to facilitating or restricting private partners in social sectors. These can be from public or private sources with varying conditions attached. Also, the balance between private and public "interest" might signal different expectations for financial/social returns from these enterprises.

Finally, the principle of a private social delivery organisation rests on having a social impact, which means the SII market in a given country is dependent on the availability of social outcome data, comparable public costs, and the present role of private finance in the delivery of social services. For a country to identify a possible "market space" for SII, data is needed for assessing the business case for across multiple sectors or social target areas. Chapter 5 presents some of this "market space" data for the G7 countries and Australia.

There are several legal and regulatory issues that impact institutional investors including the new Solvency II (insurance companies) and Basel III (banks). In addition, the EU Structural and Investment Funds (EUSIF) initiative is meant to be helpful to the social impact investment market by creating lighter regulation but may create additional barriers as decisions on how each fund will be treated will be determined at the national or local level. The legislation came into effect in the summer of 2013 and is described in further detail in Box 3.5.

Tax laws within countries have a huge impact on setting the conditions for social impact investment, primarily in terms of the rules surrounding non-profits, donations and investments. In some countries, governments have provided support to social impact investors and social sector organisations through tax credits, guarantees or subsidies. Additionally some have provided support to investees through technical assistance or procurement.

In the 2014 Budget, the UK Government announced a new Social Investment Tax Relief which will give individuals who invest in qualifying social sector organisations a reduction of 30% of that investment in their income tax bill for that year. The government's aim in introducing this new tax relief is to encourage private investment in social sector organisations (HM Government, 2013c). In 2002, the Community Investment Tax Relief (CITR) scheme was devised to encourage private investment into CDFIs. The United Kingdom has several other tax incentive schemes for investments in small and medium-sized businesses (HM Government, 2013b), including the Enterprise Investment Scheme (EIS), the Seed Enterprise Investment Scheme (SEIS) and the Venture Capital Trust (VCT).

Box 2.5. **European Social Entrepreneurship Funds**

The European Social Entrepreneurship Funds (EuSEF) regulation provides a label for investment funds that address social issues. To qualify as a EuSEF, a fund has to prove that at least 70% of the capital received from investors is invested in social businesses and that no more than 30 % of its available capital is used in the acquisition of non-qualifying assets.

For investments to qualify, the investee must not be a listed company and must have a social goal, defined as "the achievement of measurable, positive social impacts as its primary objective" clearly stated in the documents establishing the business (statutes, mission, etc…). In addition, the investee must use its profits to achieve the social goal and ensure that any profit distribution does not undermine the social goal.

The investee is considered a social enterprise if it i) provides services or goods to vulnerable or marginalised, disadvantaged or excluded persons; ii) uses a method of production of goods or services that embodies a social objective; or iii) provides financial support exclusively to social businesses as described in i) and ii).

The EuSEF regulation foresees the following social areas for social entrepreneurship:

1. employment and labour markets
2. standards and rights related to job quality
3. social inclusion and protection of particular groups
4. equal treatment, equal opportunities and non-discrimination
5. public health and safety
6. Access to and effects on social protection and on health and educational systems.

Investments can be made through a number of financing instruments such as:

equity or quasi-equity instruments

securitised and un-securitised debt instruments

units or shares of other EuSEFs (with exceptions)

secured or unsecured loans granted by the EuSEF.

A number of reporting obligations apply. In particular, EuSEFs must include in their annual report details of the social outcomes achieved with the investment policy as well as the social outcome measurement methodologies used. In addition, they must also report a number of investment-specific features, such as the:

social impact being targeted

criteria used to select the investments

risk profile

valuation and pricing methodology

methodologies used to assess social impact.

Source: Regulation (EU) No 346/2013 of the European Parliament and of the Council on European social entrepreneurship funds.

The United States also has some tax incentives in place. This includes the New Markets Tax Credits which provides a credit against US federal income taxes to taxpayers who make qualified equity investments (investments where substantially all of the equity investment is used to provide loans to, or make investments in, low-income communities). The program was authorised by the Community Renewal Tax Relief Act, which was signed into law in December 2000.[1]

Note

1. The Community Renewal Tax Relief Act can be found at: http://portal.hud.gov/hudportal/documents/huddoc?id=19129_actof2000.pdf.

References

Addis, R., J. McLeod, and A. Raine (2013), "IMPACT Australia: Investment for Social and Economic Benefit", Australian Government, Department of Education, Employment and Workplace Relations, November.

Bannick, M. and P. Goldman (2012): "Priming the Pump: The Case for a Sector Based Approach to Impact Investing", Omidyar Network, London, September.

BCG (2014), "Ready, Willing and Able: An interim review of the Investment and Contract Readiness Fund", Boston Consulting Group, London, April.

Bridges Ventures (2012), "Sustainable & Impact Investment - How we define the market", London, August.

Brown, A. and Swersky, A. (2012), "The First Billion: A forecast of social investment demand", Boston Consulting Group, London, September.

DPMC (2012) Government Response to Senate Economics References Committee Report "Investing for good: the development of a capital market for the not-for-profit sector in Australia", June 2012, www.dpmc.gov.au/publications/docs/government-response-investing-for-good.pdf, (accessed August 2014).

ECNL (2009) ECNL Study on Recent Public and Self-regulatory Initiatives Improving Transparency and Accountability of Non-profit Organisations in the European Union, April 2009.

Evenett, R. and K. Richter (2011), "Making Good in Social Impact Investment: Opportunities in an emerging asset class", The Social Investment Business, TheCityUK, October.

EVPA (2011), "European Venture Philanthropy Association: An Introduction", European Venture Philanthropy Association, Brussels, October.

Freireich, J. and K. Fulton (2009), "Investing for Social and Environmental Impact: A Design for Catalyzing an Emerging Industry", Monitor Institute, January.

GHK (2013), "Growing the Social Investment Market: The Landscape and Economic Impact" report prepared for the City of London, Big Lottery Fund, Big Society Capital, and Her Majesty's Government by ICF GHK in association with BMG Research, July.

GIIN (2013), "Catalytic First-loss Capital", New York, October.

Glänzel, G., Krlev, G., Schmitz, B. and G. Mildenberger (2013), "Report on the feasibility and opportunities of using various instruments for capitalising social innovators" TEPSIE, European Commission – 7th Framework Programme, Brussels: European Commission, DG Research.

HM Government, United Kingdom (2013a), "Achieving Social Impact at Scale: Case Studies of Seven Pioneering co-Mingling Social Investment Funds", UK Cabinet Office, London, May.

HM Government, United Kingdom (2013b), "Growing the Social Investment Market: 2013 Progress Update", UK Cabinet Office, London.

HM Government, United Kingdom (2013c), "G8 Social Impact Investment Forum: Outputs and Agreed Actions", UK Cabinet Office, London, July.

HM Government, United Kingdom (2012), "Growing the Social Investment Market: HMG social investment initiatives", UK Cabinet Office, London.

HM Government, United Kingdom (2011), "Growing the Social Investment Market: A vision and strategy", UK Cabinet Office, London, February.

IIPC (2014), "Impact Investing Policy in 2014: A snapshot of global activity", Impact Investing Policy Collaborative, November.

Jackson, E.T. & Associates (2012), "Accelerating Impact: Achievements, Challenges and What's Next in the Impact Investing Industry", The Rockefeller Foundation, July.

Koh, H., A. Karamchandani, and R. Katz (2012) "From Blueprint to Scale: The Case for Philanthropy in Impact Investing", Monitor Group and Acumen Fund, April.

Kramer, M. and S. Cooch (2006) "Investing for Impact: Managing and Measuring Proactive Social Investments", Shell Foundation, January.

Noya, A. (ed.) (2009), *The Changing Boundaries of Social Enterprises*, Local Economic and Employment Development (LEED), OECD Publishing, http://dx.doi.org/10.1787/9789264055513-en.

OECD (2000), *Social Enterprises*, OECD Publishing, http://dx.doi.org/10.1787/9789264182332-en.

OECD (2011), Financing High-Growth Firms: The Role of Angel Investors, OECD Publishing, http://dx.doi.org/10.1787/9789264118782-en.

OECD/EU (2013) Policy brief on social entrepreneurship, Luxembourg Publications Office of the European Commission.

OECD (2013b), "Innovative Financing and Delivery Mechanisms for Getting the Unemployed into Work", OECD LEED Forum on Partnerships and Local Governance, Handbook #.7, Paris, March.

OECD (2014), "Venture Philanthropy in Development Dynamics, Challenges and Lessons in the Search for Greater Impact", OECD Publishing, Paris.

Reiser, D. (2013) *Regulating Social Enterprise*, Contribution to the 2013 Columbia Law School Charities Regulation and Oversight Project Policy Conference on the "The Future of State Charities Regulation", downloaded at http://academiccommons.columbia.edu/item/ac:168586, August 2014.

Saltuk, Y., A. Idrissi, A. Bouri, A. Mudaliar, and H. Schiff (2014), "Spotlight on the Market: The Impact Investor Survey", Global Social Finance, J.P. Morgan and the Global Impact Investing Network, London, 2 May.

SIITF (2014) Impact Investment: The Invisible Heart of Markets, September.

Triodos (2014), "Impact investing for everyone: A blueprint for retail impact investing", Triodos Bank, September.

WEF (2013), "From the Margins to the Mainstream: Assessment of the Impact Investment Sector and Opportunities to Engage Mainstream Investors", World Economic Forum, Geneva, September.

WEF (2014), "Charting the Course: How Mainstream Investors can Design Visionary and Practical Impact Investing Strategies", World Economic Forum, Geneva, September.

Wilson, K. E. (2014), "New Investment Approaches for Addressing Social and Economic Challenges", OECD Science, Technology and Industry Policy Papers, No. 15, OECD Publishing, http://dx.doi.org/10.1787/5jz2bz8g00jj-en.

Wilson, K. E. and M. Testoni (2014), "Improving the role of equity crowdfunding in Europe's capital markets", Bruegel Policy Contribution Issue 2014/09, August.

Wood, D., Thornley, B., and Grace, K (2012): "Impact at Scale: Policy Innovation for Institutional Investment with Social and Environmental Benefit", Pacific Community Ventures, Institute for Responsible Investment at Harvard University and Rockefeller Foundation, February.

Annex 2.1. List of SIBs

Geography	Operational (as of 2014)	Social need	Duration (years)	Outcome payment	Investment needed/ raised
New South Wales, Australia	No	Intensive Family Support Services	5	N/A	9.2
New South Wales, Australia	Yes	New Parent and Infant Family Support	7	7+	6.4
Brussels, Belgium	Yes	Employment	2	N/A	0.2
Nova Scotia, Canada	No	N/A	N/A	N/A	N/A
Saskatchewan, Canada		Children at risk of care	N/A	N/A	N/A
Medellin, Colombia	No	Teenage Pregnancy	4-5	N/A	N/A
Rajasthan, India	No	Education	N/A	N/A	N/A
Israel	No	Prevention of Type 2 Diabetes	N/A	N/A	N/A
Israel	No	Workforce development for Arab Israeli women	N/A	N/A	N/A
Israel	No	Dropout rates from engineering studies in tertiary education	N/A	N/A	N/A
Israel	No	Recidivism	N/A	N/A	N/A
Mozambique	No	Malaria	N/A	N/A	25-30
Punjab, Pakistan	No	Primary education	N/A	N/A	25
Swaziland	No	Prevention of HIV and TB	3	N/A	10
Uganda	No	Sleeping sickness	8	N/A	20-30
Uganda	No	Secondary education	10	N/A	35
Peterborough, United Kingdom	Yes	Recidivism	8	12.2	7.6
Essex County, United Kingdom	Yes	Foster care	5	10.6	4.7

Geography	Operational (as of 2014)	Social need	Duration (years)	Outcome payment	Investment needed/ raised
Greater Merseyside, United Kingdom	Yes	Workforce development (Innovation Fund)	3	6.8	3
Shoreditch, London, United Kingdom	Yes	Workforce development (Innovation Fund)	3	4.9	1.4
Stratford, Canning Town, Royal Docks (Newham), Cathall (Waltham Forest), United Kingdom	Yes	Workforce development (Innovation Fund)	3	2.0	4.9
West Midlands (Birmingham), United Kingdom	Yes	Workforce development (Innovation Fund)	3	5.0	N/A
Nottingham City, United Kingdom	Yes	Workforce development (Innovation Fund)	3	4.4	N/A
Perthshire and Kinross, Scotland, United Kingdom	Yes	Workforce development (Innovation Fund)	3	1.8	N/A
West London, United Kingdom	Yes	Workforce development (Innovation Fund)	3	4.6	N/A
Cardiff and Newport, United Kingdom	Yes	Workforce development (Innovation Fund)	3	3.0	N/A
Greater Manchester, United Kingdom	Yes	Workforce development (Innovation Fund)	3	5.0	N/A
Thames Valley, United Kingdom	Yes	Workforce development (Innovation Fund)	3	5.6	N/A
London, United Kingdom	Yes	Homelessness	4	7.6	8
Manchester, United Kingdom	Yes	Childcare	N/A	N/A	N/A
Wales, United Kingdom	No	Foster care	N/A	N/A	N/A
Cornwall, United Kingdom	No	Aging in place	N/A	N/A	N/A
Country-wide, United Kingdom	Yes	Adoption	10	N/A	3
Illinois, United States	No	N/A	N/A	N/A	N/A
Massachusetts, United States	Yes	Recidivism	7	27	18
New York City, United States	Yes	Recidivism	4	2.1	9.6

Geography	Operational (as of 2014)	Social need	Duration (years)	Outcome payment	Investment needed/ raised
New York State, United States	Yes	Employment for formerly incarcerated individuals	5.5	21.5	13.5
National, United States	No	Workforce development	N/A	20	N/A
Massachusetts, United States	No	Homelessness	3	25	N/A
Salt Lake City, United States	Yes	Early Childhood Development	1	N/A	7
California, United States	No	Asthma Management	N/A	N/A	N/A
South Carolina, United States	No	Neonatal care (Nurse Family Partnership)	N/A	N/A	N/A
Cape Town, South Africa	No	Criminal justice	N/A	N/A	N/A

Note: This table lists all the existing or announced SIBs by geography and social need as of 18 July 2014. Figures on outcome payments and investment needed are expressed in millions of USD.

Source: Instiglio, available at www.instiglio.org/en/sibs-worldwide/, accessed on 30 August 2014.

Chapter 3

Definitions and characteristics of social impact investment

This chapter discusses the challenges related to definitions in the social impact investment market and provides a working definition based on a set of criteria for determining what might or might not be included as social impact investment. This includes a discussion of the core characteristics and definitional attributes.

3.1. Existing definitions and challenges

While in the early stages of a market's development, it can be difficult to have precise definitions, for purposes of scoping and sizing the market, it is essential to work towards a common understanding of what is meant by social impact investment and agree upon a working definition to clarify what is included and what is not. This is important for policy makers, researchers and practitioners as well as for the overall development of the market.

The term "impact investing" was coined in 2007 through an initiative coordinated by the United States' Rockefeller Foundation and its use has spread more widely since then. According to the Global Impact Investing Network (GIIN), impact investments are defined as investments made into companies, organisations, and funds with the intention to generate social and environmental impact alongside a financial return. Impact investments can be made in both emerging and developed markets, and target a range of returns from below market to market rate, depending upon the circumstances. GIIN further defines the practice of impact investing by the following four core characteristics:

- *intentionality*: the intent of the investor to generate social and/or environmental impact through investments is an essential component of impact investing

- *investment with return expectations*: impact investments are expected to generate a financial return on capital and, at a minimum, a return of capital

- *range of return expectations and asset classes*: impact investments generate returns that range from below market (sometimes called concessionary) to risk-adjusted market rate

- *impact measurement*: a hallmark of impact investing is the commitment of the investor to measure and report the social and environmental performance and progress of underlying investments.

(GIIN, 2014)

The term social investment was established in 2000 by the United Kingdom's Social Investment Taskforce and was more traditionally used in Europe until recently. In 2013, following the G8 Social Impact Investment Forum hosted by the United Kingdom, the SIITF and others involved in the international process that followed began using the term social impact investment, defined as investments made into businesses and social sector organisations, directly or through funds, with the intention of generating a measurable, beneficial social and environmental impact alongside a financial return (SIITF, 2014a).

Essentially the terms – impact investing, social investment and social impact investment – mean the same thing. For the purposes of this paper and the OECD research, which has also been part of the international social impact investment initiative, the term social impact investment is used.

At this early stage of development in the market, many players prefer to keep the definitions broad, also as a way to engage more people in the market. However, for the market to progress globally, it will be important for definitions to be clarified to make sure that there is a common language and understanding of what is considered social impact investment – and what is not. This chapter therefore seeks to deepen the discussion about social impact investing to provide a framework identifying what might or might not be considered to be SII.

3.2. Definitional characteristics, attributes and eligibility

While there is a growing consensus about the broader framing of social impact investment, there is significant debate about the definitional scope of SII. This section seeks to provide a framework for working towards a SII definition by focusing on a set of defining characteristics and attributes as well as raising questions about possible eligibility boundaries. The goal is to allow enough flexibility for the consideration of various forms of SII, while helping to clarify what might be considered to be in or out of the commonly understood meaning of SII.

A number of characteristics can be used to describe a transaction and to classify it as either corresponding to SII or not. We have identified seven key characteristics (dark blue boxes in Figure 3.1 below) which are described further in the subsequent subsections.[1] A chart of all attributes and possible eligibility boundaries for each characteristic is provided in each of the corresponding sections below and then consolidated at the end of this chapter.

The characteristics are grouped according to the SII framework components described earlier. For example, while return expectations are identified at the investor level, the measurement of social impact is typically carried out by delivery organisations. Transactions are at the centre and are the units of assessment.

Within each characteristic, suggested boundaries could help to address the variability in the definition (which attributes are in and out). It is important to note that while some characteristics have attributes that can be quantified (e.g. return expectation), others have attributes that are discrete in nature distinguishing between different classes (e.g. different social target areas). Some fall in between the two, with different classes that can be "rank ordered" (e.g. investor intent). When attributes are quantified or can be ordered, thresholds are used to decide upon what is within the scope of SII. When no ordering is possible, deciding upon what is SII or not requires selecting the eligible attributes (or "buckets") that fit within the criteria for SII.

Figure 3.1. **List of characteristics**

In dark blue boxes, grouped by SII component

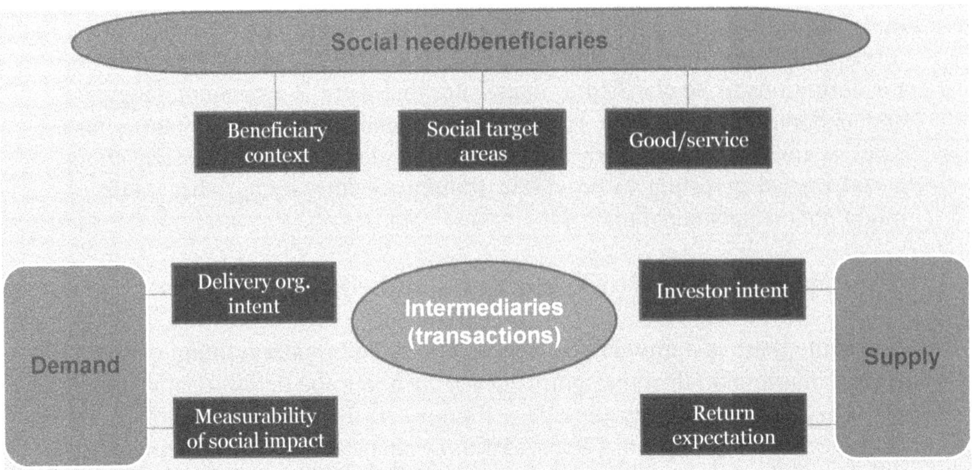

Source: OECD.

Figure 3.2 below provides two examples of characteristics, their attributes and the eligibility conditions. In the case of Social Target Areas, setting the eligibility boundaries means deciding which "buckets" are in (e.g. Education, in light blue) and which are out (e.g. Culture, in light red). With regards to return expectations, potential thresholds are also depicted in Figure 3.2 by black bars indicating that a transaction is only considered SII if returns are *expected* to be at least return of capital (black bar on the left), with an *expected* return that does not exceed the market rate of return (black bar on the right). Using this approach, investments can be classified as SII by comparing them against each characteristic and the related set of attributes and eligibility boundaries, based on a perspective of what should or should not be considered SII for each of the dimensions.

While all of the characteristics are necessary, none of them are sufficient to define SII on their own. A transaction can be considered SII only if it meets the suggested eligibility boundaries for each of the seven characteristics. Accordingly, an investment can be classified as SII if, for every characteristic, it pertains to an eligible class for those characteristics which are discrete in nature, and passes the threshold for those characteristics which can be quantified or ranked. Most importantly, these eligibility boundaries can be adjusted according to context and perspectives. For example, researchers may use a set of eligibility boundaries for data collection purposes, while a policymaker may find another set more useful for policy instrument design purposes. In addition, OECD countries may use one set of boundaries for thinking about SII while developing countries might use another. As a result, this approach allows for variation in the boundaries of SII that accommodate different purposes for defining SII. It is also important to note that some characteristics will be more relevant depending on the context and objectives of defining SII.

Figure 3.2. **Defining characteristics, attributes and eligibility**

3.2a. Social target areas

3.2a. Return expectation

Notes: The figure depicts two defining characteristics in dark blue: Social Target Areas and Return Expectation. Attributes are in light colour. Attributes in social needs provided here are examples and not an exhaustive list of all possible social needs. While returns on investment are continuous, social needs are discrete and can be thought of in terms of "buckets". Social Target Areas may overlap, but are considered here as discrete for the sake of simplicity.

Source: OECD.

As an example, if a country decides that it should introduce a tax break for social impact investments, the practical question is to decide who is eligible for such tax break. In the United Kingdom, with the recent introduction of the Social Investment Tax Relief, the boundaries were set by legal structure and size (based on employees and assets): "Charities, community interest companies or community benefit societies carrying out a qualifying trade, with fewer than 500 employees and gross assets of no more than GBP 15 million may be eligible" (HMT, 2014).

Different views exist in terms of where the boundaries lie for SII. This approach helps to explain these differences, while operationalising definitions for practical purposes such as data collection or policy implementation. Bringing all characteristics together, it is possible to devise a framework for setting clear boundaries according to the different perspectives and definitional purposes. The following sections discuss each defining characteristic in further detail.

3.2.1. Social target areas

Social target areas include a myriad of social needs in which SII can be put to work. Depending on the context, these can range from social needs, such as disability and unemployment to more traditional sectors, which applied in a certain context (see section 3.2.2) can have a high social impact.

Views on social areas to include in SII can vary according to the different perspectives of the players involved in each transaction. For example, the SIITF, which during the first year included only developed countries, focused on social issues while organisations operating in developing countries may take a broader view. GIIN is a global network seeking to attract mainstream investors to SII so for both of these reasons, they tend to categorise target areas in line with more traditional investment sectors. Figure 3.3 below provides a comparison of the social areas focused upon by the SIITF with the sectors outlined by the GIIN for global investors and intermediaries. Surprisingly, only three areas overlap (health, affordable housing and education), which illustrates how broadly perspectives can differ.

Figure 3.3. **Social needs and investment sectors**

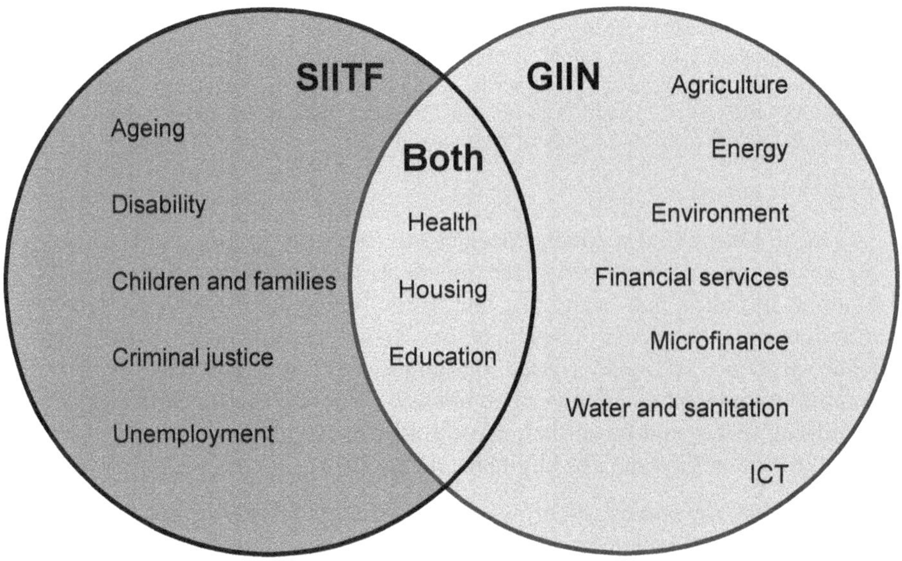

Source: OECD based on Social Impact Investment Task Force established by the G8 and GIIN website, www.thegiin.org (accessed 21 July 2014).

Table 3.1 below provides a range of social areas that could potentially be considered SII under various circumstances. The first three areas include Community, Culture and Arts, which have typically been covered by philanthropic grants. The last five include Agriculture, Energy/Environment, Financial Services, Water and Sanitation, and ICT, which can be considered more mainstream investment sectors. Therefore on both of these ends of the spectrum, inclusion as SII depends on the other characteristics of the transaction, which will likely vary by subsector or location of provision of the service (described further in section 3.2.2 below).

Table 3.1. **List of attributes for social target areas**

Characteristics	Attributes of the characteristic		Eligibility[1]
1. Social target areas	Typically philanthropy	Community	
		Culture	
		Arts	
	Core SII areas	Ageing	IN
		Disability	IN
		Health	IN
		Children and families	IN
		Public order and safety	IN
		(Affordable) housing	IN
		Unemployment	IN
		Education and training	IN
	Other areas, leaning towards mainstream	Agriculture	
		Environment and energy	
		Water and sanitation	
		Financial services (incl. microfinance)	
		ICT	

1. Eligibility used in the OECD definition for the purpose of this report. The areas not clearly listed as being core SII are context dependent (see section 3.2.2).

Source: OECD.

Dementia is an example of a social need in which SII can play an important role – this is clear from the G8 initiative launched in this area last year by the UK Active Minds (United Kingdom), which provides products and activities that help people suffering from dementia, is an example of an organisation into which investment could clearly be considered. On the other hand, the Big Idea Cooperative (United States) is a café and bookstore that focuses on reaching out to the community and selling books promoting "social, economic and environmental justice". It is a certified B-corp, incorporated as a limited liability company (LCC) and running on a not-for-profit basis. However, while providing books (literature) can be considered "culture", it is not clear that this organisation would fit within most SII definitions (including OECD) as it does not set outcome objectives and measure their achievement.

It should be noted that there is often a degree of overlap between social areas. Not only can issues cut across various social areas, but actions in one area can have an impact or spillover into other areas. Chapter 5 discusses social issues and their implications in further detail and also points to examples such as the intersection between health and ageing areas.

3.2.2. Beneficiary context

As discussed in the section above, some investment activity might target areas that would not fit within the typical SII. However by addressing the needs of populations at risk or those living in underserved or developing areas, regions or countries, some of those transactions might be considered to be SII (Table 3.2 below). Financial services can be used as an example. In developing regions, in which access to financial services may be limited, providing financial services in economically disadvantaged areas, with eventual returns on investments would be considered SII as these investments can lead to improvements in the living conditions of the population. While some of these types of investments may be considered in the sphere of development finance, they can also be considered to be in a broader definition of SII.

The same principle applies to IOT, an agriculture company which breeds sea cucumbers in Madagascar and one of the portfolio companies of Investisseurs and Partenaires, a SII intermediary (see WGIM, 2014).[2] While such a business would not be considered SII if operating in developed countries, the social dimension arising from the contribution to the fight against hunger and through the improvement of employment and living conditions for local populations, means it could be considered to meet SII criteria.

In terms of populations at risk, family type, age (life cycle needs) and other social demographics can result in social exclusion of some people. This occurs not just because of income and wealth factors, but also due to the combination of socio-demographic risks that may result in costly social exclusion if not managed or supported properly. Therefore, identifying whether populations are at risk of social exclusion due to social demographics also helps determining whether the beneficiary context falls within the scope of SII. For the purposes of the OECD definition, SII should target populations at risk.

Table 3.2. **List of attributes for beneficiary context**

Characteristics	Attributes of the characteristic			Eligibility[1]
2. Beneficiary context	Population *at risk*			IN
		Social demographics:	Age Family type Other	
		Location:	Underserved Developing Developed	
		Income		
	Population *not at risk*			OUT

1. Eligibility used in the OECD definition for the purpose of this report.

Source: OECD.

While providing affordable housing for populations at the risk of social exclusion (or *de facto* socially excluded) can have a social impact (e.g. accommodation for people that live on the streets), affordable housing that targets well-off people may improve the living conditions of the beneficiaries but not necessarily address social needs such as reducing homelessness figures. In London, a social impact bond (SIB) that aims at providing accommodation for "rough sleepers" is currently in place (see Chapters 2 and 6 for further detail on SIBs) and would fit within most SII definitions.[3]

3.2.3. Good/service

The type of the specific good or service (hereafter referred to as "good") being provided, either pure private, pure public, or mixed, is relevant to understand whether there is a market for SII. Only the two extremes (public and private) are provided in Table 3.3 for simplification. While on one extreme, a good can be classified as "public", on the other extreme it can be classified as a "private". SII eligibility will apply to goods within the continuum between the two boundaries as illustrated, for example, by the dotted black lines in Figure 3.4 below.

Figure 3.4. **Degree of publicness**

Source: OECD.

Social goods have different characteristics than pure private or public goods insofar as they would not completely exclude benefits accruing to non-target beneficiaries, but there are barriers which limit the opportunities for non-target beneficiaries to access the good without incurring any additional cost (important for the profit-principle). On one hand, goods and services that are excludable could more efficiently be provided under a fully private model. On the other hand, goods and services for which it is very difficult to exclude potential beneficiaries tend to be provided under a public delivery approach. In a list of SII attributes, each social good or service can be categorised according to its "degree of publicness" (see table 3).

Table 3.3. **List of attributes for good/service characteristics**

Characteristics	Attributes of the characteristic		Eligibility[1]
		Public	OUT
3. Good/service	Degree of publicness	(SII)	IN
		Private	OUT

1. Eligibility used in the OECD definition for the purpose of this report.

Source: OECD.

The practical use of this attribute for defining SII goods is to some extent limited, because it is challenging to accurately measure the "degree of publicness" of a good/service and fully identify the scope of the spillover effects of providing such good/service. However, this characteristic is crucial for devising policy because while a fully public good should be provided within a public model, private goods should be left for the private initiative, without any intervention of public sector authorities beyond acting upon the regulatory side.

The hybrid nature of some social goods/services might require some forms of public-private collaboration, in which some SII-like models of provision fit. The decision of whether a good is public or private or semi-public will be left to policymakers.

Table 3.4 depicts a matrix that provides a framework for further clarifying why the SII approach should be defined as between the pure public and pure private models of provision. The table builds on the expectation of SII to produce social benefits, and measures these as social outcomes (the two rows distinguish social impacts at the individual and society levels) and cost benefits, or efficiency gains (the two columns distinguish economic efficiency at the individual level from systemic/society efficiency gains).[4]

Table 3.4. **Social returns and economic efficiency**

Impacts at the individual or societal/systemic level

Degree of publicness	Individual efficiency gains	Systemic efficiency gains
Social impact on the individual	PRIVATE	Possible SII
Social impact on the society	Possible SII	PUBLIC

Source: OECD.

Two levels of "Social" are defined here: 1) the provision of goods that address the social needs of an individual or society to improve life outcomes (social impacts); and 2) the provision of goods that result in savings in the costs or improvements in the effectiveness of providing for social need (efficiency gains). The provision of goods that have no social impact is not discussed here, as they are screened out in the discussion of Social Target Areas.

Where the consumption of a good has a social impact at the individual level only (very limited spillovers) and does not result in meaningful systemic efficiency gains these are considered "private" – as the benefits/costs of the consumption is limited to the individual alone. Where the consumption of a good has both a social impact on society as a whole and result in systemic efficiency gains these are considered "public" – as their consumption is in the broadest social interest, as well as the potential for "free-riders".

Where the consumption of a good has only individual efficiency gains, but there are social returns to the society as a whole there may be space for SII; this would be the case for lowering the cost of consumption for "social impact" private goods at the individual level – such as affordable housing.[5] Where the consumption of a good creates social impact primarily at the individual level but also results in systemic efficiency gains (e.g. lowering recidivism rates, to reintegrate offenders and lower costly prison budgets) there is also potential for SII.

When the consumption of a good favours individual efficiency, but has broader social returns, it is important that any social impact spillovers are correctly factored in the SII instrument (e.g. through the use of SIBs). The consumption of affordable private goods with broad social impacts is clearly desirable, but nonetheless challenging for private enterprise models because the incorporation of externalities and monetisation of outcomes into businesses objective function is not always straightforward.

The Social Impact Bond (SIB) model is based on a "pay for success" feature that allows setting outcomes (and objectives for providers and investors) that take into account externalities. This model is described in detail in Chapters 2 and 6. As an example, the Development Impact Bond (DIB) addressing malaria in Mozambique has a clearly defined outcome measure - reducing incidence rates by at least 30%. The approach is to provide anti-mosquito nets and indoor spay to at-risk populations. By focusing on incidence rates, the DIB incorporates not outputs at the level of non-affected individuals, but also a systemic health issue.

3.2.4. Delivery organisation intent

The intent of delivery organisations can be an important characteristic in defining SII even though it is not straightforward to operationalise due to the subjective nature of the implicit attributes. A possible approach is to build on verifiable demonstrations of social intent. The intent of delivery organisations, as well as investors (discussed in a following section) is subjective and challenging to capture.

Social intent can vary from an incidental outcome (i.e. whereby a social outcome is attained despite the fact that there was no intent beforehand) to a legally binding objective (Table 3.5 below). While difficult to identify precisely, the intermediate levels in this case might be disentangled, in particular by looking at the organisation's mission and vision. Having the intention to address social challenges might not be sufficient for a social venture to be considered to be eligible for SII. For the purposes of the OECD definition, merely having the intent stated on the mission is not enough to be considered SII as the delivery organisation must put sufficient effort into demonstrating that they are committed to the social cause.[6]

A strong level of commitment can be demonstrated through some form of compulsory reporting of social outcomes to shareholders within the organisation's statutes. Within the work of the SIITF, the Mission Alignment Working Group has identified different degrees of impact intent: i) simply comply with minimum legal requirements to create impact; ii) intention to create impact and iii) a primary commitment to create impact (WGMA, 2014). Only the latter is considered to be within the scope of SII (social enterprises and "profit with purpose businesses").

Table 3.5. **List of attributes for delivery organisation intent**

Characteristics	Attributes of the characteristic	Eligibility[1]
4. Delivery organisation intent	Incidental social outcome	OUT
	Social mission intent	OUT
	Compulsory reporting	IN
	(Seeks and obtains) external certification or label	IN
	Incidental social outcome	IN
	Legally binding constraints	

1. Eligibility used in the OECD definition for the purpose of this report.

Source: OECD.

A number of initiatives have focused on developing metrics for impact assessment as well as assigning labels to companies (see Chapter 5). These help to identify companies within the scope of SII because they provide a good indication of commitment to social issues. However, while not all SII-related companies will be certified as so, some certified companies may not fully correspond to a certain definition of SII. For example, B-Corp certifies companies based on a number of variables, some of which may be considered to go beyond SII, under a narrower SII definition.

Legally binding constraints provide the strongest indication of commitment to social goals. The Financing Agency for Social Entrepreneurship (FASE) in Germany helps social entrepreneurs raise money and, in the financing contracts managed by FASE, clauses are included in order to prevent social mission drift (WGMA, 2014).

It is also important to distinguish "intent" from actions taken by companies to limit negative externalities arising from their business activity. The later should be considered Corporate Social Responsibility (CSR) and would not be included within SII.

3.2.5. Measurability of social impact

Just as with financial returns, SII investors require some form of measurement of social impact to factor both financial outcomes and social impact into their investment decisions (WGAA, 2014). This characteristic can range from the lack of measurement to formal evaluation with monetary valuations of social impact (see Table 3.6 below). Without having any form of social impact measurement a transaction cannot be considered SII.

Table 3.6. **List of attributes for measurability of social impact**

Characteristics	Attributes of the characteristic	Eligibility[1]
5. Measurability of social impact	No measurement	OUT
	Informal evaluation, not valued	OUT
	Formal evaluation but not valued	IN
	Formal evaluation and valued	IN

1. Eligibility used in the OECD definition for the purpose of this report.

Source: OECD.

Impact assessment can be carried out in a qualitative (e.g. "improved the healthcare provision"), quantitative (more robust analysis, e.g. "increased the number of patients treated that would otherwise would remain untreated") and/or by the monetisation of outcomes (e.g. attaching a value to the benefits for each treated patient as well as to the benefit to the society). It is important to attach a measure of the benefits (e.g. tangible changes in social outcome indicators or even in pecuniary terms) to impact measurement so that it is possible to understand if the workings of the delivery organisation and the investment have a *de facto* social impact.

The measurement of social impact is not straightforward, and difficulties associated with its elaboration resulted in the creation of a working group to focus on impact measurement within the process of the SIITF. The Working Group identified four main phases of the impact measurement process, hereafter "formal" impact evaluation process. First, planning requires agreement upon impact goals (including *a priori* selection of indicators) and the strategy to achieve them (see Chapter 4 for a discussion on selecting indicators). Second, building the evidence base includes collecting, storing and validating data. Third, the quality, level and efficacy of the impact are assessed based on the analysis of data gathered. Finally, the impact and the measurement process are reviewed, providing input to future improvements in impact measurement (WGIM, 2014).

In addition, a working group on impact measurement for social enterprises was created in the framework of the GECES, the European Commission's Group of Experts on Social Entrepreneurship, which released a report on "proposed approaches in European Commission legislation and in practice related to EuSEFs and the EaSI" (Clifford et al 2014).

Building on the results of these working groups and expanding the analysis to the policy dimensions of social impact measurement, the OECD (forthcoming 2015) underlined the importance of encouraging experimentation and further analysis of ongoing developments in social impact measurement by social enterprises. This could help to foster a social impact measurement culture among stakeholders. The issue of proportionality of measurement is also important. Measurement should only be done if, and to the extent that it will actually influence decision-making, and the cost of measurement is not excessive compared to the significance of that decision.

Evaluation processes are very challenging because ideally they require having a comparison group – i.e. what would have been the social outcomes if the delivery organisations would not exist. Given that running experiments and/or alternative empirical testing methodologies can be very resource intensive and require special skills, most intermediaries and companies do not take such an approach but rather use a mix of qualitative information with a range of quantitative indicators on social impact.

As an example, Investisseurs and Partenaires have a clear strategy for measuring impact (WGIM, 2014). Impact measurement does not follow an impact evaluation approach based on counterfactuals due to significant data challenges (and high costs of running experiments). Instead focus is given to impact data provided by investee companies. The impact assessment framework is nevertheless well developed (WGIM, 2014).[7]

Active Minds, briefly described above, reports the achieved social impacts on a yearly basis.[8] This report provides an overview of data regarding business activities (e.g. number of devices sold) and features the result of a survey conducted with 7% of their customers regarding the impact that the devices have had on the quality of care (for corporates) or on the life quality of dementia-suffering family members (for individuals). Even though such an approach is far from a formal and thorough assessment of social impact, it reveals awareness for the need to provide information on social impact.

The most comprehensive (but also challenging) approach to impact measurement requires a formal evaluation that also allows translating social impact into value. For example, the design of SIB contracts requires that predetermined social outcomes are attained before any payment is made by the contractor. This means that social impact needs not only to be measured but also to be valued in designing the "impact value equation" that balances the interests of outcome funders and investors (SIITF, 2014b).

3.2.6. Investor intent

Investors' social impact intent is also a characteristic that features in most SII definitions (e.g. GIIN, SIITF). As discussed above, clearly identifying intent is challenging.

On the one hand, investors can have a social impact even without having any social intent in the first place, if their investments happen to produce an unexpected or unintentional social outcome (incidental social outcome). For example, VantagePoint Capital Partners was awarded the 2013 financial investor in the cleantech industry. Investments in clean technologies create positive environmental impacts, but the main purpose of VantagePoint Capital Partners is to make profitable investments. Since there is no clear intent in achieving a social impact, such investments will not be considered as SII. Conversely, CANOPUS Foundation has been investing in solar power in Africa with a clear mission towards environmental sustainability.[9]

On the other hand, some investment contracts may formally require intentionality to achieve specified social outcomes. As an example, having a social intent may be compulsory under certain settings – e.g. within a SIB structure, the government contractor will have specific payment terms that will depend on achieved outcomes, thus requiring a legally binding social intent. Accordingly, investor intent will range from incidental outcome (which is not included in SII) to legally binding constraints (which are included).

In between these two extremes, varying levels of intent can be observed (see Table 3.7 below). For example, social intent may be expressed in a statement or other document regarding the investment made or investor profile. Citizen Capital is an investment fund that clearly states its intent to invest in social businesses and labels itself as an *impact investing* fund. The attainment of social goals is expressed in the vision as well as in a set of investment criteria that go beyond financial aspects (e.g., "investing in disadvantaged areas"; "addressing the needs of vulnerable populations").[10]

Table 3.7. **List of attributes for investor intent**

Characteristics	Attributes of the characteristic	Eligibility[1]
6. Investor intent	Incidental social outcome	OUT
	Social intent expressed in statement	OUT
	Compulsory reporting	IN
	Legally binding constraints	IN

1. Eligibility used in the OECD definition for the purpose of this report.

Source: OECD.

Foundations also have a clearly defined social mission both in statutes, as well as by legal requirements related to legal status. Some foundations have increasingly focused on SII approaches as a way to tackle social issues (Rangan et al., 2011). For example, as discussed earlier, the Gates Foundation makes Program Related Investments (PRI) in a wide variety of social areas such as education (e.g. Civic Builders), health (Global Health Fund, BiologicalE Vaccines).[11] PRI investments, which can involve a mix of instruments including debt and equity, aim to tackle social issues targeted by foundations while potentially generating some financial return.

3.2.7. Return expectation

Return expectations for investors are an important characteristic for defining the scope of SII. This characteristic is considered in most definitions being used in the SII market. In particular, there has been considerable debate regarding the risk-return profiles of SII (see WGAA, 2014). It is still unclear where the lower and upper bound of returns should stand in terms of considering an investment as SII. The last column of Table 3.8 below depicts the OECD approach to this issue. Donations stand at one of the extremes, in the sense that there is no expectation of getting part of the money back. As noted earlier, this is philanthropy and clearly cannot be considered as "investment".

Table 3.8. **List of attributes for tisk adjusted return expectation**

Characteristics	Attributes of the characteristic	Eligibility[1]
7. Return expectation	Grants	OUT
	Return of capital	IN
	Profit =< market RR	IN
	Profit > market RR	OUT

1. Eligibility used in the OECD definition for the purpose of this report.

Source: OECD.

At the other extreme, are *expectations* of profits above the market risk adjusted rate of return. On the one hand, investments made with the purpose of exceeding risk adjusted market rates of return would be no different from the mainstream for-profit market, thus not considered SII for the purpose of the working definition. On the other hand, effective rates of return on SII may turn out to be as high, or in some cases, higher than market rates of return. It is important to note, however, that investors expecting a return above risk adjusted market rates indicate that they regard such an investment to be no different from a mainstream for-profit investment and therefore it should fall outside the scope of SII. As noted earlier, rates of return vary across social sectors, and would also be taken into consideration by investors. Of course, the main issue is defining the "market rate of return" for social impact investment. To some degree, this characteristic is therefore a matter of principle in terms of the intention of the investors.

The profit distribution policy of companies can be a determinant of whether a certain flow can be considered as SII. The discussion of this characteristic has stirred significant debate – in particular, on the extent to which social enterprises should be defined by reinvesting their profits (e.g. Galera and Borgaza, 2009). Some degree of profit distribution might be needed to guarantee that investments yield positive returns. The extent to which social businesses are able to redistribute profits is also dependent upon their legal structure. For example in Italy, the legislation on social enterprises is currently being reviewed to, amongst other aspects, allow social enterprises to distribute profits (WGMA, 2014 and NAB-ITA, 2014).

3.3. OECD working definition of SII

For the purposes of this report, the OECD has sought to draw some initial eligibility boundaries for each of the core characteristics of SII. A summary of these suggestions is listed in the table below and in the draft OECD working definition of SII.

OECD Working Definition of SII:

> Social Impact Investment is a transaction between an investor and investee in a social area, targeting beneficiaries in need. Beneficiaries targeted should be at risk populations and the good provided should have a mix of public and private good characteristics. These transactions are often made using intermediaries. The investee in the transaction should, at least, inscribe a compulsory reporting clause of its social activity in the statutes, as well as provide a formal evaluation of social impact. In parallel, the investor should, at least, have a compulsory reporting clause for social impact investments and have return expectations above or equal to zero, but not above the market rate of return (actual return may be higher).

As discussed earlier, while all of the characteristics listed in the chart below are necessary, none of them alone are sufficient to define SII. A transaction can be considered SII only if it meets the defined eligibility boundaries for each of the seven characteristics.

Table 3.9. **List of characteristics, attributes and eligibility**

Characteristics	Attributes of the characteristic			Eligibility[1]
1. Social target areas	Typically philanthropy		Community	
			Culture	
			Arts	
	Core SII areas		Ageing	IN
			Disability	IN
			Health	IN
			Children and families	IN
			Public order and safety	IN
			(Affordable) housing	IN
			Unemployment	IN
			Education and training	IN
	Other areas, leaning towards mainstream		Agriculture	
			Environment and energy	
			Water and sanitation	
			Financial services (incl. microfinance)	
			ICT	
2. Beneficiary context	Population *at risk*			IN
		Social demographics:	Age	
			Family type	
			Other	
		Location:	Underserved	
			Developing	
			Developed	
		Income		
	Population *not at risk*			OUT
3. Good/service	Degree of publicness		Public	OUT
			(SII)	IN
			Private	OUT

Characteristics	Attributes of the characteristic	Eligibility[1]
4. Delivery organisation intent	Incidental social outcome	OUT
	Clear social mission intent	OUT
	Compulsory reporting	IN
	(Seeks and obtains) external certification or label	IN
	Legally binding constraints	IN
5. Measurability of social Impact	No measurement	OUT
	Informal evaluation, not valued	OUT
	Formal evaluation but not valued	IN
	Formal evaluation and valued	IN
6. Investor intent	Incidental social outcome	OUT
	Social intent expressed in statement	OUT
	Compulsory reporting	IN
	Legally binding constraints	IN
7. Return expectation	Grants	OUT
	Return of capital	IN
	Profit =< market RR	IN
	Profit > market RR	OUT

1. Eligibility criteria used in the OECD definition for the purpose of this report.

Source: OECD.

Notes

1 . Other characteristics could possibly be used. However, these seven characteristics are necessary and sufficient to: i) identify the SII "space" in the economy; ii) cover all SII players (and the profiles) relevant for a definition and iii) discuss the scope for policy action.

2 . Further information can be obtained through I&P's website, available at: www.ietp.com/entrepreneurs_en/#profil.

3 . Further information on the London "rough sleepers" SIB can be found at: https://www.london.gov.uk/priorities/housing-land/tackling-homelessness-overcrowding/rough-sleeping/social-impact-bond-for-rough-sleepers.

4 . Please note that these should not be regarded as dichotomous but rather as vectors flowing from the individual to the societal/systemic levels. There is also a parallel deliberately implied here with spillovers and externalities as well as with macro and micro impacts.

5 . In the United Kingdom, the percentage of the population living in households where the total housing costs (net of housing allowances) represent more than 40% of disposable income (housing cost overburden rate) was almost 41%, well above the EU average of 25% (OECD, 2013c, p. 61).

6 . Please note that the combination of social intent expressed in the mission combined with, for example, a formal measurement and valuation of social impact should be duly considered

7. Further information about Investisseurs and Partenaires is available at www.ietp.com/. The impact measurement report can be found at: http://ietp.com/our-esg-impacts-annual-report-online.

8 The report can be retrieved from Active Minds website at: www.active-minds.co.uk/index.php.

9. Further information about VantagePoint Capital Partners can be found at: www.vpcp.com Further information about CANOPUS Foundation is available at: www.canopusfund.org.

10. Information on Citizen Capital can be found at: www.citizencapital.fr/.

11 . Further information available at: www.gatesfoundation.org/how-we-work/quick-links/program-related-investments.

References

Addis, R., J. McLeod, and A. Raine (2013), "IMPACT Australia: Investment for Social and Economic Benefit", Australian Government, Department of Education, Employment and Workplace Relations, November.

Clifford J, Hehenberger L, and Fantini M (2014), "Proposed approaches to social impact measurement in European Commission legislation and in practice related to: EuSEFs and the EaSI", http://ec.europa.eu/internal_market/social_business/docs/expert-group/social_impact/140605-sub-group-report_en.pdf.

Galera, G., and C. Borzaga (2009), "Social enterprise: an international overview of its conceptual evolution and legal implementation", *Social Enterprise Journal*, 5(3): 210-228.

GIIN (2014), Global Impact Investing Network website, www.thegiin.org/cgi-bin/iowa/resources/about/index.html (accessed 15 May 2014).

HM Government, United Kingdom (2013c), "G8 Social Impact Investment Forum: Outputs and Agreed Actions", UK Cabinet Office, London, July.

HMT (2014), "Social investment tax relief guidance", HM Treasury, London, March, https://www.gov.uk/government/publications/finance-bill-2014-legislation-explanatory-notes-and-guidance.

NAB-ITA (2014), "La finanza che include: gli investimenti ad impatto sociale per una nuova economia", National Advisory Board Report, Italy, Social Impact Investment Taskforce established by the G8, September.

OECD (2013c), *OECD Economic Surveys: United Kingdom 2013*, OECD Publishing, http://dx.doi.org/10.1787/eco_surveys-gbr-2013-en.

OECD/EU (forthcoming 2015), "Policy Brief on Social impact measurement for social enterprises EU Commission/OECD, Luxemburg", Publication Office of the European Union.

Rangan, K.V., S. Appleby, and L. Moon (2011), "The Promise of Impact Investing", Harvard Business School, Background Note No. 512-045, Boston.

SIITF (2014), "Impact Investment: The Invisible Heart of the Markets", Social Impact Investment Taskforce, London, September.

SIITF (2014b), Social Impact Investment Taskforce Report, Policy levers and Objectives – Explanatory Note for Governments, London, September.

Thornley, B., D. Wood, K. Grace and S. Sullivant (2011), "Impact Investing: A Framework for Policy Design and Analysis", Pacific Community Ventures, Institute for Responsible Investment at Harvard University, and Rockefeller Foundation, January.

WGAA (2014), "Allocating for Impact: Harnessing private capital for public good", Working Group on Asset Allocation (WGAA), Social Impact Investment Taskforce established by the G8, September.

WGIM (2014), "Impact Measurement: Shifting the Paradigm", Working Group on Impact Measurement (WGIM), Social Impact Investment Taskforce established by the G8, September.

WGMA (2014), "Profit with Purpose", Working Group on Mission Alignment (WGMA), Social Impact Investment Taskforce established by the G8, September.

Chapter 4

Context setting: Differences in social needs and service delivery across selected countries

This chapter looks at the context for social impact investment across the G7 and Australia. This includes looking at changes in social needs and direct public sector provision over time as well as a discussion of the different models of social service provision in each country. This chapter covers: a review of trends in social needs in key service sectors (health, employment and education, housing, criminal justice and family services); trend changes in public spending in the above areas; models of social services provision; evidence of best practice in this area; and, methods and issues for measuring social impact.

4.1. Introduction

The contexts in which Social Impact Investment (SII) takes place, country-to-country, will have a significant bearing on the potential for SII to have a lasting and positive role in society. Key contextual factors include: the extent to which present legislation and financial regulation plays a role in facilitating social impact investment; the extent of social need by sector; the evolving size and role of public intervention, also by sector; varying models of social service provision in each country, stakeholders and their present effectiveness; and, the political economy of private intervention.[1]

The variation in these contexts can inform how different SII approaches may be more appropriate in some sectors than in others, and easier to implement in some countries than in others. The purpose of this chapter is to contribute to the discussion of how SII could fit in to present forms of social impact investment by mapping key social-contextual factors in the G7 and Australia.

4.2. Social outcomes and social spending

The space in which SII could take a positive role in social development provides further contextual information for assessing the need for SII, and its likelihood to have a meaningful and lasting effect. *Understanding how different countries achieve preferred social outcomes, relative to the extent of public social interventions, is important for gauging this "SII market space"*. Of course, the final "market space" will also be determined by the extent to which SII might want to go "above and beyond" the public efficiency and effectiveness, but because governments are the largest investor in social causes in every country, the specific role of public spending relative to key social outcomes is the most appropriate starting point for such an estimate.

Below, two sections will discuss trends in social outcomes and public expenditure from across a range of social sectors, with a focus on what these data might mean for SII.

4.2.1. The need (for better) social services: trends in social outcomes

The extent to which any investment can make a social impact will rely on the type and extent of need – and demand for improvement – across an array of social outcomes. Social outcomes are evolving in different directions, in different social sectors, for different reasons – and social services can take a supporting role in both positive and negative settings. For instance, increasing life expectancy and ageing societies increase demand for long-term care of various kinds (frailty, dementia, in-home or institutional care), whereas the increase in single-parent families or families in which both parents work will need to be facilitated by family care services in preschool and after-school.

The following subsections provide some examples of evolving needs in health, employment and activity (including education), housing, public order, and family service sectors.

4.2.1.1. Health and care needs of the elderly

Although there are many health outcomes and services to consider across the population, the long-term health care needs of the elderly are of particular interest for the SII discussion for two reasons. First, the health of the elderly is an important social consideration as societies age, and people live and work longer. Second, because it is here where the highest voluntary private social spending occurs because of the intersection of health and old-age spending (OECD, 2014a).

Figure 4.1. **One in 20 over 60's have dementia, on average one in 8 over 65's are subject to long-term care, and in the next 30 years rates the support ratio for older people will halve**

Panel A: Population aged 65 years and over receiving long-term care, 2011 (or nearest year) and prevalence of dementia among the population aged 60 years and over, 2009

Panel B: Over 65 population as a ratio of working age population (15-64)

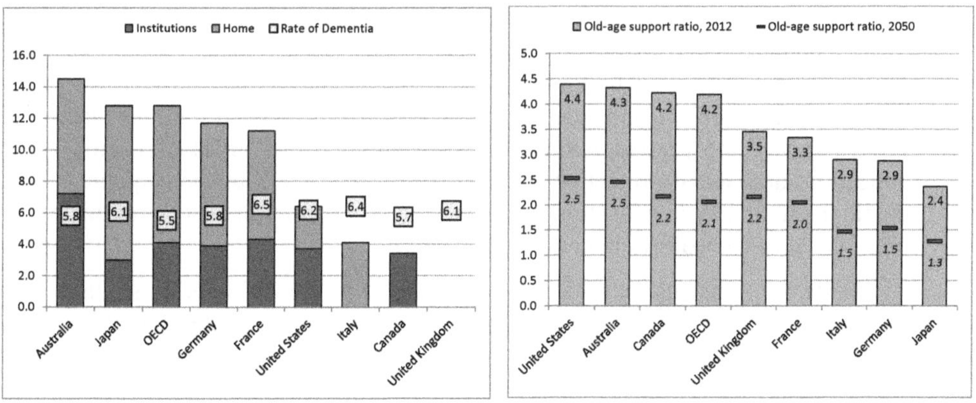

Note: For long-term care estimates, data is missing for the United Kingdom, and is for different dates in other countries (Japan [2006], United States [2007], Canada [2009], and France [2010]). The long-term care OECD average is for 21 countries (see online data annex). For prevalence of dementia, OECD average is for 34 countries.

Sources: OECD Health Statistics 2013 (OECD, 2013d), (http://dx.doi.org/10.1787/health-data-en and citing Wimo et al. [2012] for dementia estimates) and Society at a Glance, (OECD, 2014b).

Figure 4.1 reports on the extent of social need for elderly care, and predictions for social need in the future. Panel A maps the rates of people aged 65 years receiving long-term care at home or in institutions (bars), and plots over these figures the prevalence of dementia among the population aged 60 years and over. The demand for elderly long term care (LTC) in OECD countries is high, with 1 in 8 people over 65 receiving LTC, two-thirds of whom are receiving this care at home. Long-term care needs are determined by health needs, and so by using the example of dementia – a concern for old age in particular, resulting in progressively high-intensity health and care supports – it can be estimated that at least half of LTC receivers over 60 will need some high-intensity services at some point in their lives.[2]

The juxtaposition of the figures in Panel A, read alongside the evidence in Panel B, gives the strongest message for the need for innovative social delivery organisations in these countries. First, although LTC provision varies widely, the demand for these provisions is likely to be very similar across countries – and so there is unmet demand. Second, as the scale of dependency increases, demand for care will increase substantially relative to the working-age population in the coming decades.

4.2.1.2. Unemployment, inactivity and school drop-outs

Helping people into good quality and secure employment is critical for a range of desirable social outcomes today and in the future. Today, the private and public social gains from employment include a reduction in household poverty – and the improved quality of life this brings – increases in productivity, and reductions in benefit dependency. For tomorrow, employment is critical for building the social contributions needed to pay for a person's own pension and elderly care, as well as for tax contributions that fund much of the present public social spending in the areas of health, education, and social protection among others. Helping youth into quality employment or stay in education settings is the foundation for success in this area, as well as a healthy economy and society.

Table 4.1 presents experiences of long-term unemployment spells, unemployment rates for older workers, education drop-out rates for older youth, and rates of inactivity in youth (NEET – "not in education, employment or training") in younger and older cohorts. Percentage point movements up or down in the past five years are presented in parentheses, where available. Altogether, the data highlight need, and to a degree a lack of effective policy development, in present social "activation" systems: two factors which would indicate demand for SII-type innovation in this sector.

More specifically, many country systems are struggling to produce effective employment or "activation" outcomes in older youth cohorts, and, with the exception of Germany, people who are unemployed are facing much greater challenges in returning to work now than they did five years previously (Italy and Japan have notable challenges to contend with here, and across the OECD as a whole the rate of longer term unemployment has increased by 50% in five years).

Table 4.1. **Although younger and older cohorts have experienced little change in unemployment risks, more unemployed people are out of work for a year or more**

	Long-term unemployment (2013)	Unemployment (55 to 64 years, 2013)		Dropout rates for youth aged 20-24 (2011)	NEET rates (2011)	
		Male	Female		15-19	20-24
Australia	19.2 (4.4)	4.3 (0.6)	3.2 (0.3)	13.9	7.8 (1.4)	11.7 (1.0)
Canada	12.7 (4.9)	6.9 (-1.1)	5.8 (0.1)	8.3	7.7 (0.5)	14.6 (0.9)
France	40.4 (5.1)	7.5 (1.1)	6.5 (0.5)	14.5	7.1 (0.8)	20.3 (2.4)
Germany	44.7 (-0.8)	6.2 (-1.8)	5.3 (-2.8)	12.1	3.5 (-0.7)	12.6 (-2.7)
Italy	56.9 (12.5)	6.7 (2.9)	4.1 (1.4)	20.5	11.4 (1.2)	28.4 (5.8)
Japan	41.2 (12.7)	4.4 (-1.0)	2.8 (-0.5)	...	10.1 (2.5)	...
United Kingdom	36.3 (11.8)	5.4 (-0.5)	3.8 (0.9)	12.4	9.5 (-1.2)	19.1 (1.1)
United States	25.9 (9.7)	5.6 (-1.5)	5.0 (-1.0)	9.0	7.1 (0.8)	18.5 (2.3)
OECD countries	35.3 (11.6)	6.1 (-0.1)	5.0 (0.0)	15.0	8.2 (0.1)	18.5 (2.4)

Notes: Employment figures are rates in given years, figures in parentheses record the difference in the rates compared to five years previously. Dropout rates are for the share of 20-24 year-olds having left school and not holding an upper secondary degree.

Sources: OECD dot.stat employment and education series, 2014c; OECD, 2014d.

Figure 4.2. **Australia has the most success in activating low skilled youth**

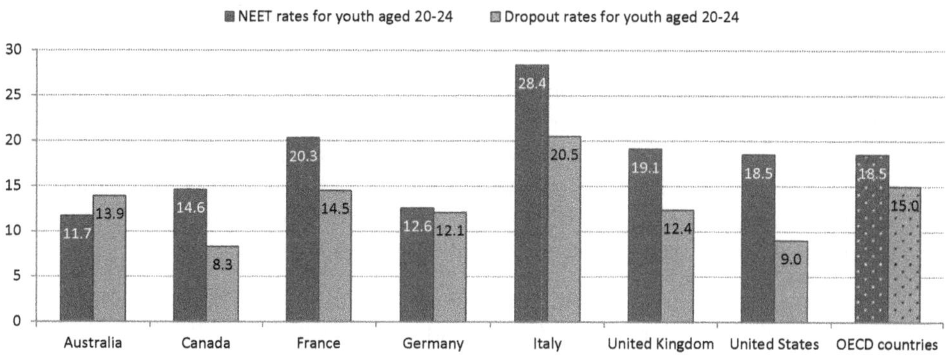

Notes: Both series are for 2011. Data for Japan are missing. Dropout rates are for the share of 20-24 year-olds having left school and not holding an upper secondary degree.

Sources: OECD dot.stat education series, 2014c; OECD 2014d.

Educational dropout rates also represent a variable challenge across countries and a predictor of hard-to-place inactive youth; preventing dropouts from education is realistic and measureable intervention space for SII, with as many as 1 in 7 older youth not leaving school with only a lower-secondary. Figure 4.2 maps the NEET rates for older youth to the dropout rates, and shows that in all cases, with the exception of Australia, it is unlikely to be low education alone that inhibits the activity of youth as NEET rates outstrip drop-out rates. In Canada, Italy, the United Kingdom and the United States the difference might suggest an unmet demand for services to place qualified youth into work.

In the area of employment support, a number of countries are encouraging SII through the introduction of Social Impact Bonds (SIBs), including one to reduce youth unemployment in the United Kingdom, see Chapter 4 for details.

4.2.1.3. Housing affordability and quality

A further sector related to important social outcomes is housing. Providing all members of society with a secure and good quality accommodation is not only a human right and an ethical priority, but stable good-quality homes provide the foundation from which stable employment is achieved, families are formed, communities are built, local environments are protected, and social cohesion can develop.

Figure 4.3 presents two panels of housing data from the Gallup World poll and shows overall, that while there has been some falls in the rates of dissatisfaction with housing options over recent years, these have generally been from high levels (on average over 1 in 3 respondents in the OECD reported dissatisfaction with the level of good quality affordable housing in the city or area where they lived). At the same time, respondents also reported an increase in experiences of being unable to meet hosing costs.

Across the OECD, almost one in ten people have trouble meeting housing cost at some point in the year, in Australia this is now as low as 1 in fifty, and nearer 1 in 7 in the United States (where the financial crisis would have had an effect). The message for SII is that there remains high demand for affordable housing in most countries, as well as for services to improve the quality and affordability of present housing stock (although to a lesser extent).

An example of how SII can meet demand for affordable housing comes from the United Kingdom's Tesco Supermarket chain which recently responded to debates on housing needs (as well as changing demand form their customer base) by unlocking it's land banks for housing projects (reportedly including their own GBP 1 billion house-building project [see Guardian, 2014]). Contributions to housing stock, particularly when unlocking banked land, should contribute to macro-social goals for increasing available, and in turn affordable, housing stock (for a detailed discussion of the range and definitions of what constitutes a social impact investment see Chapter 4).

Figure 4.3. **Satisfaction with affordable housing increased in recent years, but experiences of difficulty in meeting costs also increased**

Panel A: dissatisfied with affordable housing 2008, 2012

Panel B: recent difficulty providing adequate housing

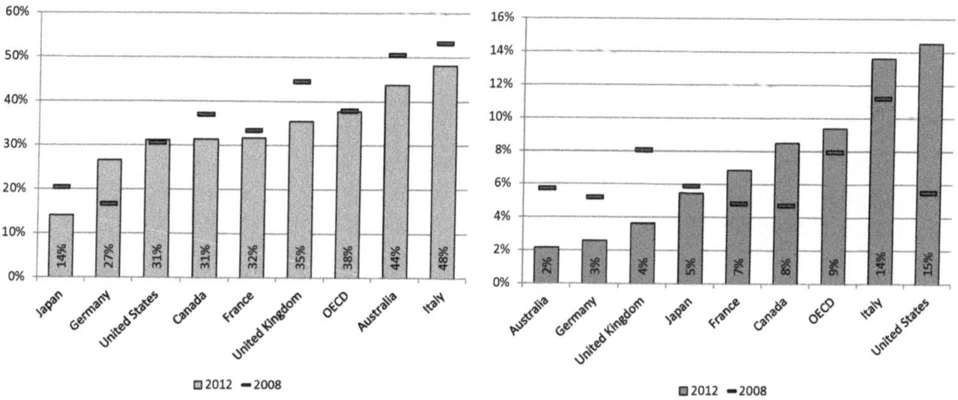

Notes: The Gallup World Poll was conducted by telephone in approximately 140 countries in total, and all OECD countries, using a common questionnaire translated into the main national languages. Samples are nationally representative of the resident population aged 15 and over in the entire country, including rural areas in most cases. Sample sizes are limited to around 1 000 persons in most countries (exceptions include Iceland and Luxembourg [c. 500]; Japan and New Zealand [c. 750]). Data for Germany and Japan are the average of four quarterly samples. Observed data points on each trend line are "filled", estimates are "empty". Panel A records the proportion of respondents reporting being dissatisfied with the level of good quality affordable housing in the city or area where they live. Panel B records the proportion of respondents who answered "Yes" to the question "Have there been times in the past twelve months when you did not have enough money to provide adequate shelter or housing for you or your family?".

Source: Gallup World Poll, 2014.

4.2.1.4. Policing, safety and crime

Crime is a blight on societies, and depending on the severity of the crime experienced, can have severe personal and social impacts. Reducing crime and the fear of crime are major social goals, and whether present systems are coping with expectations or not will provide an insight as to whether SII has a role in this sector.

Crime statistics are difficult to interpret accurately because they often rely on crimes being reported, and convicted, and this may result in important variations in different countries (and in turn national-level reporting biases). For this reason nationally-relative measures of contact with the police are report in Table 4.2, and show that although numbers are rising overall, and in France and Italy (but not for Italian juveniles), most countries report lower rates of people being in formal contact with the police since the mid-2000s.

Whether increases in contact with the police are a proxy for improvement in policing, and an improvement in overall safety is generally open to debate (lower rates might equally be due to higher risks and lower policing standards), and so indicators of safety and policing are also reported in Table 4.2. Results for confidence in policing and feeling safe in your locality would suggest that increased contact with police in France does not proxy a worsening social situation. In fact, across all countries, both confidence in the police and feeling safe in the locality at night have improved (with the exception of small falls in the latter indicator in Italy and Japan). For SII, although social outcomes seem to be improving in this sector, innovation may still be required, because progress is slow in many countries, and on average three in ten people still report feeling unsafe outside at night or not having trust in the police.

Table 4.2. **Indicators of policing safety and crime trending in the right directions, but still have some way to go**

	Confidence in local police between 2007 and 2012		Do you feel safe walking alone at night in the city or area where you live?		Persons brought into formal contact with the police and/or criminal justice system, all crimes (Index 2004=100)		Prison rates of over 18s per 100 000	Prison occupancy rates
	2007	2012	All	Juveniles	2007	2012	2011	c.2013
Australia	78	80	...	...	77.2	84.3	167.1	96.0%
Canada	88	87	97	89	77.5	82.6		96.4%
France	73	74	112	134	66.6	78.2	131.4	116.8%
Germany	76	82	...	...	64	76.1		82.4%
Italy	74	76	118	93	75.3	74.8	132.5	128.8%
Japan	70	74	83	67	72.5	72.3	65.8	77.2%
United Kingdom	69	76	...	...	63.1	68		111.2%
United States	78	78	89	73	57.9	67.9	939.5	99.0%
OECD	70	72	106	105	68.3	72.2	193.8	...

Notes: For crime rate changes OECD average is an average of data for 23 countries. For prison rates ("Prisons, Penal Institutions or Correctional Institutions" means all public and privately financed institutions where persons are deprived of their liberty. The institutions may include, but are not limited to, penal, correctional, and psychiatric facilities under the prison administration. "Persons Held" should exclude non-criminal prisoners held for administrative purposes, including persons held pending investigation into their immigration status and foreign citizens without a legal right to stay held prior to removal) Canadian data is for 2010. Prison occupancy rates United Kingdom data is for England and Wales only, data for Australia, England and Wales, France, Germany, and Italy are from 2013; 2012 in Japan and the United States, and 2009 in Canada.

Sources: Society at a Glance (OECD, 2014b); citation of sources: Gallup world Poll, 2014 and United Nations Office on Drugs and Crimes (UNDOC - www.unodc.org/). For prison occupancy rates author's calculations of national informant data (available on request).

Finally, prison rates and prison occupancy rates are interesting indicators of social outcomes for the SII discussion because recidivism was the first social outcome to be linked to a social impact bond (recidivism data is not available due to problems with comparability across countries – see Richardson, 2009). The standout case in this picture is the United States, where prison rates are five times higher than the OECD average. Providing for prisoners is a costly process, and so innovation in crime/recidivism prevention services will be in general demand, which may create a space for SII products. Moreover, when prisons are over their capacity (above 100% occupancy rates – see Figure 4.4) this signals a pressing unmet demand for these services, or even alternative services to incarceration.

Figure 4.4. **Prisons in France, Italy and the United Kingdom are overfull**

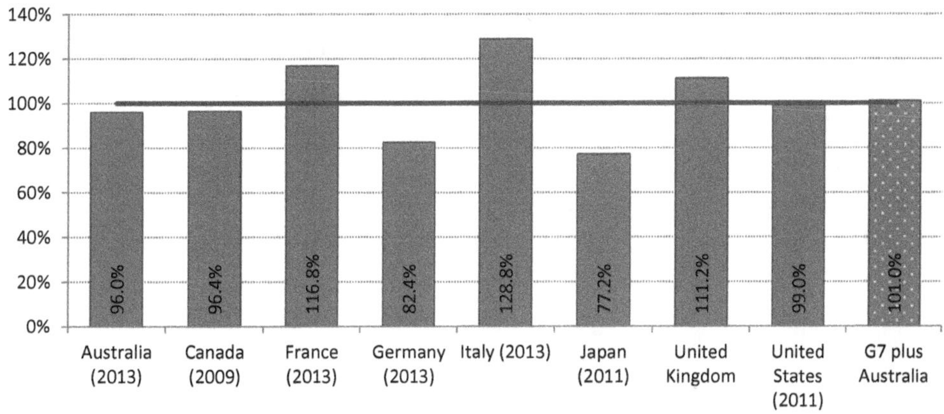

Notes: Prison occupancy rates United Kingdom data is for England and Wales only. Data for Australia, England and Wales, France, Germany, and Italy are from 2013; 2012 in Japan and the United States; and 2009 in Canada.

Source: Author's calculations of national informant data (available on request).

4.2.1.5. Family care and the employment of women

The social value of childcare for child development, family formation and female employment has been recognised for many years (OECD, 2011a), and has been supported by increases in public investment in this area in many OECD countries before the crisis (ibid) and one area of family policy that has seen expansions during the crisis period (OECD, 2014a). Childcare is also seen as an important contributor to the efficiency of social systems, preparing children for later schooling, increasing productivity in adulthood and reducing the likelihood of anti-social outcomes (see for instance Heckman and Masterov, 2007). Related to the provision of childcare, and important for achieving important gender equity goals for societies, is helping women access good quality secure employment.

Table 4.3 presents data on recent developments in childcare enrolment and prime-age female unemployment and part-time employment (Figure 4.5 maps female part-time employment to preschool enrolment). Together these data point towards changing demand for childcare services, as well as changes to childcare take-up, yet a general message is hard to interpret because the expected finding of an increase in childcare for both age groups is not reflected in positive changes to broad employment patterns for women of prime working age. Nonetheless, some country-specific findings can inform the SII discussion, including: a suggestion of a need for innovation in non-childcare support for unemployed Italian women, and an expansion in the provision of childcare in the United States, where there is likely to be unmet need in the pre-school years (3-5) in particular (see Figure 4.5).

Figure 4.5. **In countries where there is low childcare enrolment and low part-time employment, there is likely to be unmet demand for childcare**

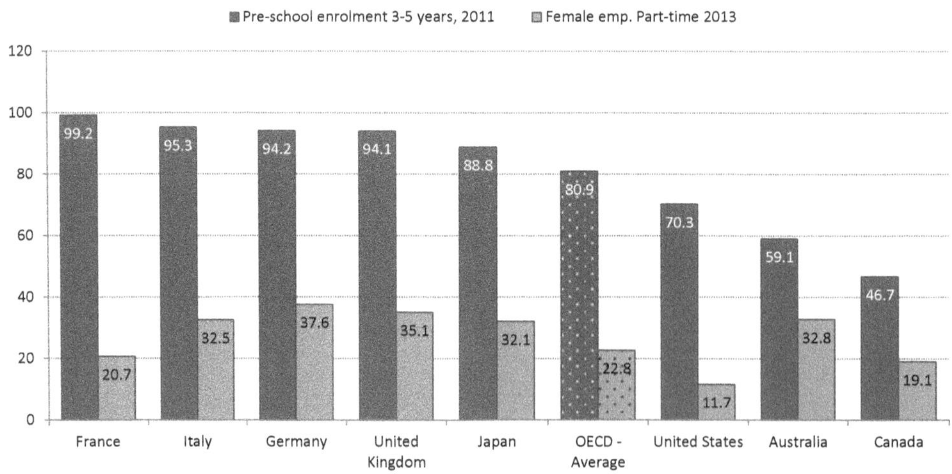

Sources: OECD dot.stat, education and employment series and the OECD Family database (both 2014e); Health Behaviour in School-aged Children Study (2010).

Another “family” social need of interest for SII is children in out-of-home care. Supporting these children has the potential for large social impacts in terms of providing secure, supportive, and long-term home environments that maximise the child’s development opportunities and also reducing costs associated to institutional care (public and private). Table 4.3 presents rates of "looked after" children per 1 000 children aged 11 to 15 and shows that Italy and France have almost twice as many children in foster or child homes than the OECD average. Examples of SIBs already at work in this area, in the case of adoption in the United Kingdom and support for "looked after" children in Australia, however it must be stressed that care for the most vulnerable children should prioritise quality of placement over quantity of placements, and be carefully monitored for children's living standards following placement.

Table 4.3. **Cross-nationally, changes in aggregate childcare enrolment do not map to female (un)employment figures**

	Pre-school enrolment rate children aged 3-5		% children < 3 in formal childcare and pre-school		Women – part-time employment		Women – unemployment rate		Children 11-15 in foster or child homes (per thousand)
	2007	2011	2006	2010	2009	2013	2009	2013	2010
Australia	54.9	59.1		33.2	33.9	32.8	4.6	4.7	
Canada		46.7			19.8	19.1	6.1	5.6	11.4
France	100	99.2	42.4	48	21.2	20.7	8.2	8.7	14.1
Germany	91.2	94.2	13.6	23.1	39.1	37.6	6.9	4.6	4.4
Italy	98.3	95.3	28.6	24.2	30.2	32.5	8.5	12.4	17.4
Japan	88.7	88.8	22.5	25.9	30.5	32.1	4.9	3.9	
United Kingdom	89.8	94.1	39.7	42	35.1	35.1	5.2	5.6	5.7
United States	59.1	70.3		43.2	13.6	11.7	7.2	6.3	3.5
OECD average	77.4	80.9	28.8	32.6	22.7	22.8	7	7.5	7.4

Sources: OECD dot.stat, education and employment series and the OECD Family database (both 2014e); Health Behaviour in School-aged Children Study (2010).

4.2.2. The evolving size of the public share: Public social expenditure by sector

There are a number of important reasons to introduce the size and type of public expenditure on social interventions for the SII discussion. First, how much public bodies in different countries presently spend on social interventions can be considered an indication of the revealed willingness to invest in social impact measures. Second, comparing spending amounts by sector can be used as a proxy for assessing the size and priority of different social impact investment "markets" (prior to factoring-in the ambitions of SII). Third, comparing social spending across countries alongside social need can be used to highlight cost efficiency issues in the public sector, leading to an indication of the extent of need for innovation and new approaches, such as SII.

A number of dichotomies are important for understanding how SII, in its different forms, might fit into public service management: large companies and SMEs, cash and service benefits, and national and local markets and governance. Across these dichotomies there are links; with larger companies more likely to be involved in cash investments or financial services (insurance, micro-finance) rather than services which are more often managed at the local government level and within the potential remit of small to medium sized enterprise.

4.2.2.1. Government spending: Where the money goes

Figure 4.6 maps government expenditure in the areas of social protection, education, health housing and public order (each linked to a social outcome area measured above) and clearly shows that human and social services account for the majority of government expenditure across OECD countries. The different ways in which public sector services are financed will inevitably result in different challenges for reform. For instance, where public benefits are financed though social contribution payments, recipients are likely to expect predefined conditions of delivery to be met (rates of payments, services standards, or services providers themselves) years into the future. Compared to services financed through general taxation, the contribution conditions are more likely to challenges to innovation.

Social protection alone makes up one third of total government expenditure on average, and is over 40% of total government expenditure in France, Germany Italy and Japan. Social expenditure includes old-age care and pensions, as well as payment to families for childcare (family allowances and childcare, but not education), and unemployment and social assistance payments. Education and health also make up a large part of government spending, with around USD 1 in every USD 4 going to these services across the OECD. In countries where social protection spending is relatively low, like Australia and the United States, education and health spending is higher. Over the three sectors of social protection, heath, and education each country spends around 60% to 70% of its budget.

Small but socially-relevant interventions of "housing and community amenities" and "public order and safety" top up the expenditure on social interventions by around 5-8% of total. France stands out as a country with relatively high housing expenditure, whereas the anglophone countries are spending more of total on public order and safety.

Other research has mapped the trends in government expenditure, and shows that across the OECD as a whole, the biggest falls over the last decade came in the areas of general public services and to a lesser extent defence. Health, social protection, and economic affairs show the biggest relative increases (OECD, 2011b).

Figure 4.6. **Social protection, health, housing and education account for over 60% of total public spending**

Structure of general government expenditures by function (2011)

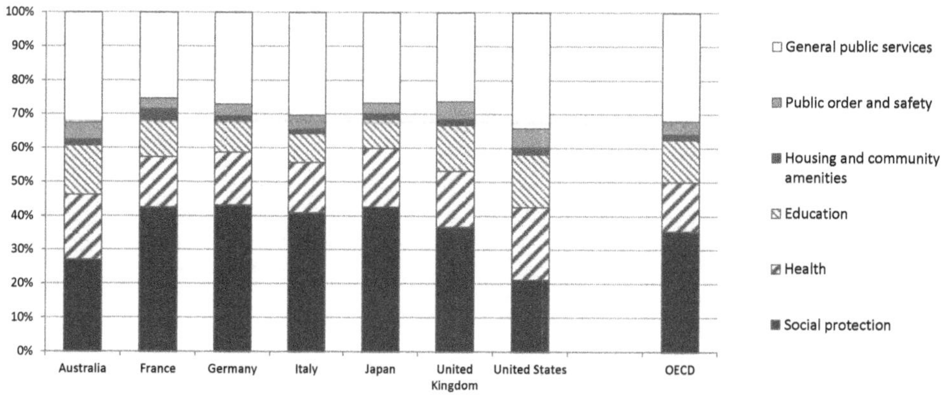

Notes: "General public services" includes general services, and spending on defence, economic affairs, environmental protection, and recreation, culture and religion. Canada is missing due to incomplete expenditure data. OECD average is for 30 countries (Chile, Mexico and New Zealand also missing).

Sources: Government at a Glance, 2013e analysis of *OECD National Accounts Statistics* (database). Data for Australia are based on *Government Finance Statistics* provided by the Australian Bureau of Statistics.

An idea of the "openness" of public services by sector to third party interventions can be gleaned from available estimates of the extent to which the public sector is co-producing[3] in these sectors. An OECD survey of 26 countries in 2011 (OECD 2011b – Brazil, Egypt, Russia and the Ukraine plus 22 OECD countries) mapped "significant" civil society involvement in the delivery of public series and showed that of 58 examples of co-production, 19% were in social protection, 16% were in housing and community amenities, and 10% were in each of the areas of environmental affairs, economic services, education and health. In each sector, co-production in service delivery was found at all levels of governance (local, state and federal or national levels - ibid: 23).

4.2.2.2. Trends in social protection spending in cash and in-kind

The following section explores the evolving market space for SII by breaking down available government expenditure trends in total social protection, housing and health spending in terms of service provision and cash spending. The purpose here is to get a better idea of changing demand for social services, as it is in this area that SII might be possible for entrepreneurs from small, medium and large enterprises alike.[4]

Figure 4.7 maps the trends in cash spending and service expenditures in each of the G7 countries and Australia between 1996 and 2011. Across all OECD countries, on average, cash spending was falling pre-crisis only to pick-up again with increasing demand for low-income cash benefits following 2009. In contrast, service spending has been steadily increasing.

Figure 4.7. **Expenditure trends show services are taking up more of the social protection budget, in some case exceeding cash spending**

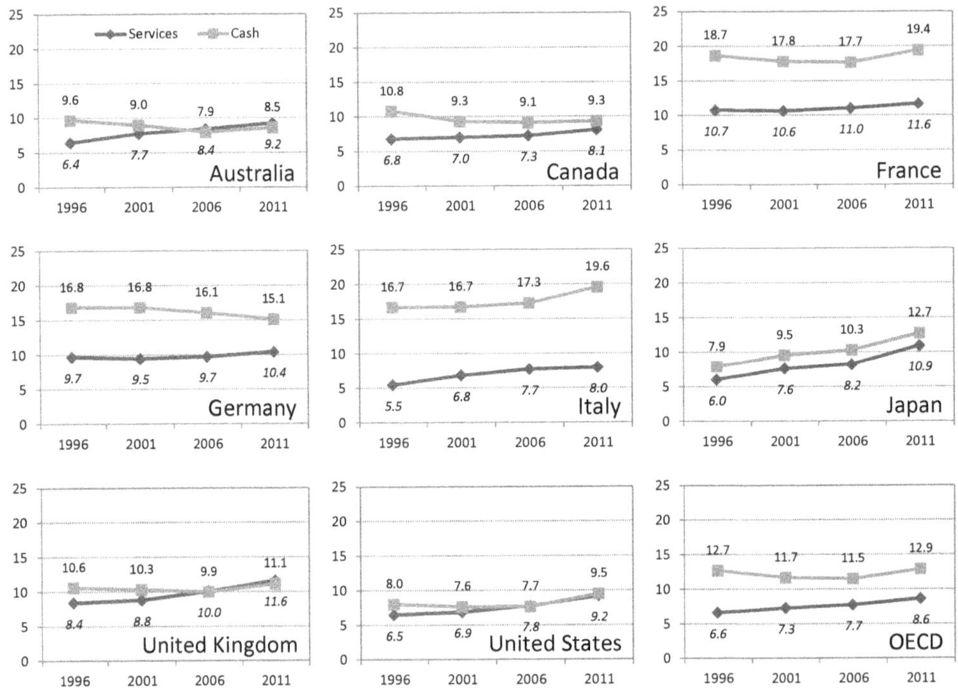

Notes: Data report aggregate public social protection spending by type and do not include private social expenditure or education expenditure (public or private), but do include housing and health spending. Data for 2011 are provisional. Service spending reflects running costs of public services, cash spending reflects the value of cash transfers without administrative costs. OECD average is for 34 countries.

Source: OECD Social Expenditure Database, 2014a.

Not all countries follow the OECD trend however. Australia, Canada and Germany (the latter being a traditionally high cash spender) have all seen rates of cash spending fall over the period, whereas Italy and Japan have seen marked increases in cash spending. In regards to services, all countries with the exception of France and Germany have seen increases in expenditure of at least 1-2% of GDP or more. Service spending has increased by close to one-third in Australia and the United States, and almost doubled in total in Japan.

Although there is not much difference in service expenditure across the countries, three broad expenditure groupings are clearly shown here. The European countries of France, Germany and Italy are high spending countries, favouring cash expenditures. The Anglophones are lower-spenders but are more balanced by type, to the point where in Australia, the United Kingdom and the United States, expenditure levels are now favouring services. Finally, Japan is reporting stable upward trends across both spending types.

A limitation with Figure 4.7 is that it does not break down the social expenditure by sector, which is an important task for the SII discussion because of the different sector-specific challenges to this type of social entrepreneurship. For instance, one driver of the shift to greater service delivery overall is likely to be demographic change. In the area of social protection there are generally high rates of service intervention for the preschool years and end of life care, compared to higher rates of cash intervention across childhood as a whole, and into employment and living supports in adulthood (tax credits, minimum income guarantees and so on).

Figure 4.8. **In most countries old-age spending is growing, in Australia and Japan, services are increasingly used**

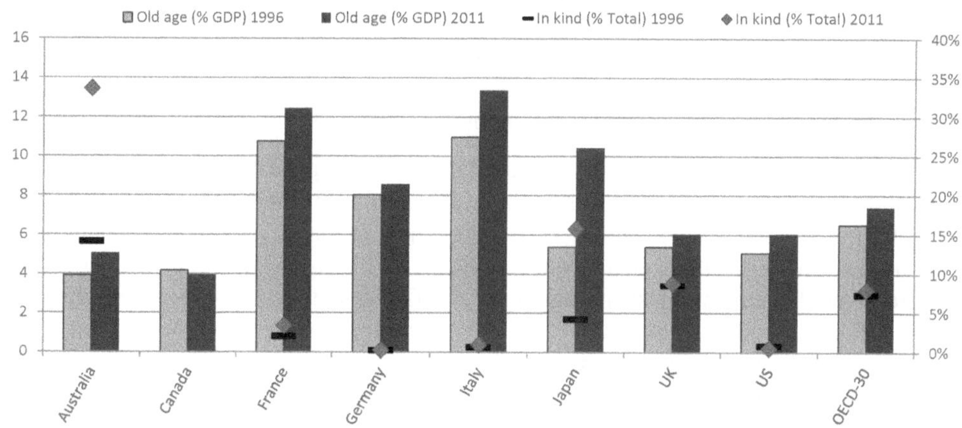

Note: Left-hand axis is for % of GDP, right-hand axis is for in-kind spending as a percentage of total spending (see Table 4.4).

Source: Author's calculations of OECD Social Expenditure data, 2014a.

Figure 4.8 above and Table 4.4 below introduce the breakdowns of spending types by sector, as well as trends of these breakdowns, for the G7 and Australia (covering old-age spending, health, housing, family and [un]employment). Results clearly show that increases OECD-wide in old-age, health, and family, and no consistent reductions elsewhere across all countries (a small drop in overall unemployment spending). In old-age, all countries with the exception of the Germany and the United States have seen both increases in overall spending and service spending, although in some cases this is small. The change in old age spending is likely to reflect the increasing need for elderly long-term care (personal and household services) as populations' age.

The OECD's social expenditure database also maps private (or non-government) social expenditures – where finances are managed by private bodies (Adema et al, 2011) – and shows that aggregate mandatory private and voluntary private spending by sector are highest for old age and health. Mandatory private spending refers to "social support stipulated by legislation but operated through the private sector, e.g., direct sickness payments by employers to their absent employees…" whereas voluntary private spending refers to monies managed through "privately operated programmes that involve the redistribution of resources across households" via collective support arrangements (see Adema et al., 2011c, 93:94 for more details).

Perhaps surprisingly, voluntary private spending outstrips mandatory spending in all countries (with the exception of Italy – total voluntary spending is almost four times as high at 2.3% of GDP on average in 2011) and Old Age interventions (via pension contributions, at 1.3% of GDP on average) generally receive more voluntary private investment than health (with the exception of France, Germany and the United States via health insurance and pharmaceutical purchases). Notably for social enterprises, particularly in what might be small to medium sized enterprises, service interventions play a very small role in private social expenditure.

Across the OECD as a whole, total education expenditures from public and private sources are also rising (as well as in all of the G7 countries and Australia, with the exception of France and Germany – see online data annex, and Education at a Glance [OECD, 2013c]). On average in 2010, total public education spending in the OECD countries stood at 6.3% of GDP compared to 5.4% of GDP in 1995. It is important to note however, for interpreting where space may exist for SII, these education figures do not disentangle private spending – whether promoted through mandatory systems, paid by families, or paid by local voluntary or professional services – from public spending. In most countries private spending is small relative to public and will more likely go to fees and variable costs associated with education provision (educational items, books and so on), and not fixed capital costs (buildings and their up-keep and wages) that public funds cover. SII may look very different in education space depending on which type of education service is being provided, and which market will provide the custom (private or public). Further breakdowns might be made in future research, and some countries will be more affected by this than others, including Japan where private education spending is higher-than-average.

Table 4.4. **Old-age and health spending dominate public social protection budgets, and have been increasing in almost all countries**

		Australia	Canada	France	Germany	Italy	Japan	United Kingdom	United States	OECD-30
Old age	1996	3.9	4.2	10.8	8.0	11.0	5.4	5.4	5.1	6.5
		14.1%	*n.d.*	*2.0%*	*0.2%*	*0.6%*	*4.2%*	*8.5%*	*0.8%*	*7.3%*
	2011	5.0	4.0	12.5	8.6	13.4	10.4	6.0	6.0	7.4
		33.6%	*n.d.*	*3.3%*	*0.2%*	*0.9%*	*15.7%*	*8.7%*	*0.5%*	*7.9%*
Health	1996	4.6	5.8	8.0	7.8	5.1	5.3	5.3	5.8	4.9
		...	...	...	...	...	...	...	...	...
	2011	5.8	7.2	8.6	8.0	7.0	8.2	7.7	8.0	6.2
		...	...	...	...	...	...	...	...	...
Family	1996	2.8	0.8	2.7	2.0	0.7	0.5	2.3	0.5	1.8
		21.2%	*13.8%*	*42.1%*	*37.8%*	*35.3%*	*62.4%*	*20.8%*	*52.9%*	*27.8%*
	2011	2.8	1.2	2.9	2.2	1.5	1.4	4.0	0.7	2.2
		31.3%	*17.9%*	*57.7%*	*44.6%*	*50.2%*	*34.8%*	*34.6%*	*87.3%*	*43.1%*
(Un)employment	1996	1.7	1.6	2.9	2.9	1.0	0.8	1.1	0.5	1.9
		31.3%	*28.4%*	*41.9%*	*44.1%*	*34.9%*	*38.8%*	*34.8%*	*32.3%*	*32.2%*
	2011	0.8	0.9	2.5	2.0	1.2	0.6	0.8	0.9	1.6
		35.9%	*25.6%*	*37.2%*	*40.1%*	*33.9%*	*47.2%*	*51%*	*13.8%*	*35.8%*
Housing	1996	0.2	0.6	0.9	0.3	0.0	0.0	1.7	n.d.	0.4
		...	...	...	...	...	...	...	n.d.	...
	2011	0.3	0.3	0.8	0.6	0.0	0.1	1.5	n.d.	0.4
		...	...	...	...	...	...	...	n.d.	...

Notes: Cells in white report the total public spending by year on each sector as a proportion of GDP, shaded cells report the proportion of this spending delivered in services with the exception of (un)employment where shaded cells represent the proportion of total spending on active labour market policies. "n.d." is for no data, and "..." replaces 100% for health and housing services where total spending matches total service spending. 2011 data is provisional.

Source: Author's calculations of OECD Social Expenditure data, 2014a.

4.2.2.3. Limitations of the data and appropriate interpretation of the data by sector

Social expenditure figures are taken from the OECD Social Expenditure Database (SOCX), education spending figures are taken from OECD Education Database. In theory all government expenditure should be in the Social Expenditure Database; however it is easier to collect federal spending than regional or local spending because state governments or devolved authorities do not always report to national governments how the money they managed is being spent (that which is raised, or devolved through block grants or other mechanisms). In practice this may mean social expenditure data may not fully represent all spending in countries where money is managed independently at local or regional levels.

Correct interpretation of the spending figures is important for accurate estimation of the need, and the potential boundaries, for SII – and so some caution is required. In some cases, missing spending is more likely to be found in some benefit types and sectors rather than others. For instance the Swiss and US federal systems allow for parental and maternity leave benefits to be provided by cantons or states, and as such are examples of where family spending can be missed, and cash-based interventions under stated. Yet, issues to do with missing expenditure are not restricted to federal countries or cash benefits. In the Netherlands for example, block grant expenditure from central to local government can hide additional spending on children as municipalities provide the childcare support, and they may finance this service out of the general block-grant made to municipalities.

Finally, social expenditure figures do not cover administrative costs (particularly in cash) or spread the value of large one-off costs (buildings for instance), which in both cases mean that annual estimates represent an underestimation of the total public cash or service intervention.

4.3. Models of social service provision: Who does what and how?

Having looked at the broadly at the potential market space for SII, this section looks in more detail at how governments are presently meeting the demand for social services.

4.3.1. Practices in public social service delivery

In practice, the process of public social service delivery is not too different from providing services in the private sector. Simply put, the delivery cycle of a social service includes a planning stage, delivery process and review. In more detail: planning covers when service decisions are made (the "gap in the market" or "social need" is indicated), and the services are planned and designed; the delivery process involves commissioning services or service delivery by public employees; and, the review process involves service evaluation and service re-design (OECD, 2011b).

In the majority of cases the process of delivery is a cycle; unless a new need is identified or system innovation is undertaken (this can be driven by effectiveness or efficiency reasons). Recently, two factors have driven the need for innovation in social services delivery, the first being increased demand for multiple services in the most vulnerable populations, and the second being reductions in available resources driven following the onset of the financial crisis and global recession (OECD, 2015).

Innovation in social services, increases in demand, and pressures to lower public budgets all point towards a potential role for new models in delivering social services, including a potential role for social enterprises. However, the nature of public service delivery can create specific challenges to social enterprise involvement, and so are salient to the SII discussion, such as:

- **Governance**: whether services are managed and financed at the central, regional or local level, or even a combination can mean many actors, with different political and financial pressures, influencing the service delivery methods and desired social impacts. Complex forms of governance can create different challenges for private social service delivery organisations joining the social market space particularly in the case of integrated social services, discussed below.
- **System planning**: Public interventions are designed to fit into systems, meaning complementary public services are considered in the design. SII will exist in a system of complementary public services which may be relied upon to regulate demand for an SII service, or facilitate outflow from a service (e.g. social protection will limit/regulate the inflow of homeless people into an SII homeless service, and homeless treated with SII may benefit from public employment services on exit). These complementary services will inevitably impact on the achievability of social impact goals set for an SII, and may create sustainability risks.
- **"Cross-sectoral" returns and "wrong" pockets**: Related to system planning are the possibilities for cross-sector returns, which for SII may mean returns ending up in the "wrong pockets" (see OECD, forthcoming). Where public finances control multiple sectors, systems planning can allow for returns to accrue in *sector A* from interventions undertaken in *sector B*. Moreover, not all returns will need to be tracked or monetised, in the public system, or achieved within a pre-determined timeframe – in each case an important challenge for SII reporting.

- **Fixed capital and human capital**: At present, in many countries, public service systems have large banks of fixed capital and many employees. These bring hidden costs to social service spending (rates in Figure 4.5 report running costs), but can also represent additional policy options (with social outcomes) for governments if the location of the service and the employment conditions therein are part of national plans for employment creation, retention and safe employment. Both costs and purposes can result in a small market space and lower liquidity of public funds for private social delivery organisations.
- **Borrowing, funding streams, and sustainability**: Public services are backed by nations and traditionally have had access to borrowing or funding streams to allow for the treatment of social need even in the most difficult economic circumstances. They do not have a profit principle, meaning they can trade-off low cost cases with cases business might see as too costly to work with. Critiques of SII highlight the profit-principle which may "trump" social efforts at the individual or community level if the business model becomes unsustainable (Yunus cited in Esposito, 2013).

Meeting these challenges effectively is essential for the general SII business case, as well as for the SII business case by sector (where these issues can be more or less important). The following sections address both the governance issues and issues with gaps in public service, data, evaluations and measuring social impact. For the other points there is no further discussion, but this should not detract from their importance, or the need for effective solutions.

4.3.2. The governance of public benefits and budgets

Table 4.5 records the level of governance involved in the delivery of services in the sectors of social protection, employment services, housing, health, education, and public order. Where data is available, each country row records the level of governance at which social services are managed by sector.

At first glance this table highlights the complexity of social service delivery across the G7 countries and Australia, with all countries involving different government levels across the sectors, sometimes mixing government stakeholders within sectors, and involving multiple stakeholders in a single service area in just over one-third of cases (40 out of 112 examples, sometimes including private providers). Australia, France, Japan and the United Kingdom have the most centrally-managed services, Australia and Canada have many regionally-managed services (state or provincial level), and local government is involved in 7 settings out of 12 in Germany. The United States has by far the most tiered settings, with no area involving fewer than two government partners.

Table 4.5. **The governance of social services is complex and varied across countries**

	Social protection		Employment		Housing		Health			Education			Public order	
	Social Assistance	Family cash benefits	Job centres (& Job training)	Cash benefits	Institutions (homeless, children in care)	Social Housing	Secondary health services	Primary health services	Mental health / counselling services	Compulsory	Childcare	Adult Education (lifelong learning)	Policing	Prisons
Australia	C/F	C/F	C/F	C/F	CF, R	CF, R	R	R	R	R	R	R	CF, R	R
Canada	R	CF, R	C/F (from 2017)	C/F	…	R	R	R	R	R	R	R	CF, R, L	C/F
France	R, L	CF, R	L	C/F, L	R	C/F	R*	R*	R**	C/F	R, L	C/F	C/F, L	C/F
Germany	R	C/F	L	CF, R	L	R, L	R, L	Pr. with R, L	R, L	R	L	R	C/F	R
Italy	R, L	C/F	R	C/F	…	L	R	R	R	R, L	R, L	…	C/F, L	C/F
Japan	L	L	…	C/F	…	…	C/F, L	C/F, L	C/F	L	L	C/F	C/F, L	C/F
United Kingdom	C/F	C/F	C/F	C/F	L	L	CF, R	CF, R	CF, R	C/F, L	C/F, L	…	R	**C/F (Pr).**
United States	CF, R, L	CF, R	CF, R	CF, R	CF, R, L	CF, R, L	**Pr. with CF, R*** **	**Pr. with CF, R*** **	**Pr. with CF, R*** **	CF, R, L	CF, R, L	C/F, L	R, L	**CF, R (Pr.)**

Notes: C/F is central or federal, R is regional (referring to states, provinces or counties), L is local (municipalities, local governments, city governments), Pr. denotes private provider involvement. Data is provisional.

Sources: OECD, correspondence with national-expert reviewers.

A number of issues for the SII discussion can be derived from the above. First, SII by sector will involve different business models by country, designed to "fit" into pre-existing public models, and so transferability of good SII practice will therefore need to be assessed accordingly. Second, the complexity of systems and number of stakeholders in public settings is likely to limit the size of social enterprise start-ups generally, as the potential of co-production to scale will be limited or otherwise transaction costs may be high. Third, where sector investment and sector impact are not aligned in terms of management (primary health services improving school attendance in the United Kingdom for instance) additional challenges to measuring assessing the value an impact, and delivering reimbursements, will be additionally complex creating further transaction costs. Fourth, private enterprise is already a notable co-producer in the United Kingdom and the United States (cases are highlighted in bold in Table 4.5), the examples of which can inform practices in other countries. Finally, in some cases, the management and the resources by sector will not be aligned, for instance when central government block grants pay for local level service delivery (including outsourcing), which can create uncertainty and risk in regards to sustainability of SII funding sources, complementary public services, and the expectations for the social impact made by any given SII.

Evidence on how public resources are shared between levels of governance is shown in Figure 4.9. Using the example of Canada, on the top right-hand side of the figure, shows that sub-centrally derived revenues (y-axis), at below 60%, are lower than the proportion of total government expenditure undertaken at the sub-central level (x-axis) at over 60%. This means that some central government funding is being devolved to the sub-central level for administration (around 10% of total). All countries under the 45 degree line receive devolved funds to some degree. Notably, in Australia and the United States sub-central governments only administer their own revenues; in Japan, some sub-central revenues are administered at the central level.

For SII, as noted above, not only will this shift of funds create levels of uncertainty about streams of revenue etc. to social enterprise where it exists, but the information on the share of revenue administered at different levels highlights the potential for SII to function differently in different countries (nationally administered services will have different "business" plans compared to locally administered services, for example in the areas of fixed capital and employee "banks", economies of scale, underlying legislation and reporting/auditing mechanisms).

Figure 4.9. **How much of central government funds are devolved to local authorities for social interventions varies widely**

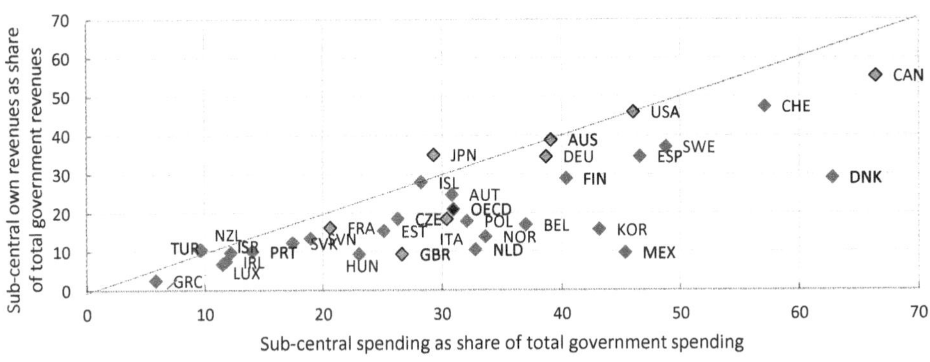

Note: G7 countries and Australia are highlighted.

Source: OECD (2013b).

4.4. Evaluating what works in social service provision

The evidence on social outcomes and social spending shown sections 4.2 and 4.3 can be used to highlight challenges and opportunities for SII. However, together these only highlight the space into which SII might move, and they do not provide any clear messages as to how to implement processes that might "fill these social outcome gaps".

This section reviews briefly the mix of evidence on good practice in public service provision in the area of elderly care and childcare, highlighting potential opportunities for SII. What is most evident is that better data and evaluations are needed. Chapter 6 discusses briefly ways to address this gap, and provides a point of departure for meaningful outcome measurement for impact evaluation in this area.

4.4.1. Good practice in service provision

Reading the data on social outcomes above alongside the data on public interventions clearly shows continued and sometimes expanding social need in the context of increases of public spending in most social sectors. In particular, the areas of elderly care and childcare stand out as priorities. For SII to make a meaningful contribution to these areas it is important to have an understanding of what makes for good practice in these areas.

4.4.1.1. Services supporting long-term elderly care: what works?

Increasing demand for long-term care of the elderly in many OECD countries is putting increasing pressures on many public budgets through increasing health costs (and creating social care service and pension needs) and this is projected to almost double in most countries over the next 3 decades. For these reasons integrated care services for the frail elderly have received much attention from policymakers in recent years. Below are some examples of integrated care practices and their social outcomes evaluations (focussing on reduction in hospital care) for the frail elderly:[5]

- A longstanding integrated care service for the over 75's in Canada (the *Programme of Research to Integrate the Services for the Maintenance of Autonomy* or PRISMA) coordinates integrated care provision through a joint governing board, and in some cases, pooled funds. A Randomised Controlled Trial (RCT) evaluation of PRISMA found reduced functional decline of programme participants, more satisfaction with their care, and reduced likelihood to re-use emergency department services ten days after discharge (Hebert et al., 2005).
- Two small integrated care pilot programmes, *Rovereto* and *Vittorio Veneto,* were undertaken in in two provinces in Italy in the 1990s and provided integrated community-based medical and social services to the elderly. Evaluations of both programmes showed reductions in acute hospital admissions, and positive health outcomes amongst programme participants (MacAdam, 2008).
- In Victoria, Australia, the *Hospital Risk Admission Programme* (HARP) pilot provided services to elderly people who regularly attended hospital

emergency departments. Through engagement with the elderly person's carer, case management, multi-disciplinary teams, and outreach, the service achieved a reduction in emergency department admissions (of 20.8%), inpatient care (of 27.9%) and number of bed days for inpatient care (of 19.2%) (Bird et al., 2007).

- In England, in 2008, the *Integrated Care Pilots programme* (ICPs) involved number of organisations integrating the care of older people with long-term conditions (via case management or care planning) for the purpose of lowering the risk of hospital admission. The evaluation of these two-year pilots showed decreases in planned admissions, outpatient service use and process improvements (e.g. use of care plans, professional training – without associated measurable social outcomes), but no increase in patient satisfaction was recorded, and there was no reduction in emergency department admissions (RAND, 2012).
- Services delivery practices that were successful at reducing high cost emergency services use and hospital care included involving the elderly person's carer (HARP), case management of individuals, service planning and single point of entry to multiple service providers (all examples with the exception of ICPs), multi-disciplinary teams (HARP and *Rovereto/Vittorio Veneto*), screenings or assessments (PRISMA, *Rovereto/Vittorio Veneto*), outreach (HARP), service coordination boards (PRISMA).

Integration practices are gathering momentum in OECD countries as political interest in cost effectiveness grows – meaning SII and private social delivery organisations can embrace these approaches, and find solutions to the specific challenges of working in complex governance settings.

4.4.1.2. Services supporting families with young children: what works?

Services to support families represent a different type of "investment" expenditure and clear links with later life outcomes (in some cases creating returns decades after an intervention). Relative to the "treatment" of frailty in old-age, family supports are an investment designed to "prevent" children from being unprepared for school, the economy and society. Moreover, there is evidence of unmet demand for childcare in different countries of the OECD, as well as evidence of increasing public commitment to family services in every country in relative terms (the exception is Japan, where overall family spending has tripled, and although absolute level of family service spending has increased, this is relatively lower than cash spending).

Service interventions for families and children in France, the United Kingdom and the United States that have been subject to RCTs, show that:[6]

- Nurse-family partnerships and home health visits providing pre- and post-natal care for low income mothers and their infants in their own homes in New York, Memphis, and Washington produced positive gains in intended child well-being (including educational outcomes) and parenting outcomes including parenting practices (Greenberg and Shroder, 2004).
- Integrated childcare interventions in the United States (North Carolina's Abecedarian programme and Michigan's Perry Preschool), although relatively small (109 and 123 participants, respectively) produced large, long-term gains in education and health. These results have persisted over several decades, and in the case of the Perry Preschool service, early childcare also produced benefits in adult income and employment (Schweinhart and Weikart, 1993; Schweinhart, 2003).
- Evaluations of general family supports had mixed outcomes, with positive outcomes from the French intervention in Créteil that actively engaged parents and school to remedy truancy and disciplinary issues, and the Carrera programme in the United States which offered integrated support services to teenagers to improve educational engagement. Among the other family support interventions aimed at providing services for parent and child well-being, there were few benefits. Practices here included: case management and integrated service delivery (US Comprehensive Child Development Programme), home visits by "supportive listeners" or community groups (British Social Support and Family Health Programme), and case management to teen mothers (the Young Families Can, Phoenix, United States) (OECD, 2015).

Mobile home health units, and delivery of services in the home were successful in producing the desired social outcomes due to benefit of home service that reduce service take-up barriers (affordability, motivation etc.) and the chance it provides to professionals to gauge the full extent of the family living conditions and needs (McKeown, 2000). Childcare practices were successful where multiple integrated services (e.g. education, nutrition, health) are provided in childcare settings for the most at-risk children and less successful where fewer at-risk families took up the service (see OECD, 2104f). Finally, for more general family service interventions, successful interventions included engaging with parents in the school (for truancy and discipline), and less successful interventions included comprehensive support (parent and child well-being), case working (teen pregnancy) and supportive listening (maternal and child health – see OECD, 2015).

Some key messages for SII here include: the highest social returns are found in the most vulnerable groups, although these groups will often require more intensive services; returns on social interventions in childhood may take many decades to come to fruition; and, providing services in people's homes, and to family units, creates unique opportunities for tailoring care to specific needs.

Notes

1. Historical factors also play a role, but are beyond the scope of this paper.
2. As noted earlier in the paper, the G8 has put a special spotlight on the issue of dementia and has been investigating the role that SII can play in helping to address this growing social concern.
3. The OECD report defines co-producing as "a way of planning, designing, delivering and evaluating public services which draw on direct input from citizens, service users and civil society organisations" (OECD, 2011b). This definition differentiates between voluntary involvement citizens and services users and civil society organisations (including via contractual and semi-contractual obligations) and formal contracting or outsourcing, services to the private sector (which are not included here).
4. Although there may be a role for SII in the provision of cash transfers (pensions, social insurance [maternity pay or hospital costs for childbirth] or micro-credit) these are high-risk large-scale areas more suitable for larger social enterprises.
5. The following evidence is summarised from OECD 2015, Chapter 3, section 3.5.
6. The following evidence is summarised from OECD 2014g, Chapter 3, section 3.4.

References

Adema, W., P. Fron and M. Ladaique (2011), "Is the European Welfare State Really More Expensive?: Indicators on Social Spending, 1980-2012; and a Manual to the OECD Social Expenditure Database (SOCX)", OECD Social, Employment and Migration Working Papers, No. 124, OECD Publishing, http://dx.doi.org/10.1787/5kg2d2d4pbf0-en.

Bird, S., Kurowski, W., Dickman, G K, Kronborg, I. (2007) "Integrated care facilitation for older patients with complex health care needs reduced hospital demand" *Australian Health Review August 2007 Vol 31 No 3.*

DPMC (2012) Government Response to Senate Economics References Committee Report "Investing for good: the development of a capital market for the not-for-profit sector in Australia", June 2012, downloaded at www.dpmc.gov.au/publications/docs/government-response-investing-for-good.pdf, August 2014.

ECNL (2009) ECNL Study on Recent Public and Self-regulatory Initiatives Improving Transparency and Accountability of Non-profit Organisations in the European Union, April 2009.

Esposito, R. (2013) The Social Enterprise Revolution in Corporate Law: A Primer on Emerging Corporate Entities in Europe and the United States and the Case for the Benefit Corporation. *William and Mary Business Law Review*, Vol.4, Issue 2, Article 7.

Gallup World (2014) Gallup World Poll.

Greenberg, D. and M. Shroder (2004), *The Digest of Social Experiments: Third Edition",* The Urban Institute Press, Washington, DC.

Guardian (2014) *Tesco Unlocks its Landbank to Build 4,000 New Homes*, August 2014, www.theguardian.com/business/2014/jul/18/tesco-unlocks-landbank-to-build-4000-new-homes.

HBSC (2010) Health Behaviour in School-aged Children Study.

Hebert R, Tourigny A, Gagnon M (2005) "Integrated Service Delivery to Ensure Person's Functional Autonomy" Canada: Edisem Inc.

Heckman, J. J, and Masterov, D. (2007) *The Productivity Argument for Investing in Young Children*, NBER Working Paper. No. 13016, Cambridge.

MacAdam, M. (2008) "Frameworks of Integrated Care for the Elderly: A Systematic Review" *CPRN Research Report, April 2008.*

OECD (2011a) *Doing Better for Families*, OECD Publishing, Paris.

OECD (2011b) Together for Better Public Services: Partnering with citizens and civil society, OECD Publishing, Paris.

OECD (2013d) *OECD Health Statistics 2013*, http://dx.doi.org/10.1787/health-data-en.

OECD (2013e) Government at a Glance, OECD Publishing, Paris.

OECD (2013c), *Education at a Glance 2013 – OECD Indicators*, OECD Publishing, Paris, http://dx.doi.org/10.1787/eag-2013-en.

OECD (2014a) *Social Expenditure database*, OECD Publishing, Paris.

OECD (2014b) *Society at a Glance*, OECD Publishing, Paris.

OECD (2014c) *OECD dot.stat: employment series*, OECD Publishing, Paris.

OECD (2014d) *Investing in Youth: Brazil*. OECD Publishing, Paris.

OECD (2014e) *OECD Family database*. OECD Publishing, Paris.

OECD (2015), Integrated Service Delivery for Vulnerable Groups.

RAND (2012) "National Evaluation of the Department of Health's Integrated Care Pilots: Final Report" *RAND Europe, Ernst & Young LLP, prepared for the Department of Health, March 2012.*

Reiser, D. (2013) *Regulating Social Enterprise*, Contribution to the 2013 Columbia Law School Charities Regulation and Oversight Project Policy Conference on the "The Future of State Charities Regulation", downloaded at http://academiccommons.columbia.edu/item/ac:168586, August 2014.

Richardson, D. (2009) Extreme Poverty and Vulnerability on OECD Countries: A Scoping Paper. OECD DELSA-ELSA-WP1 (2009)6.

Schweinhart, Lawrence (2003), "Benefits, Costs, and Explanation of the High Scope Perry Preschool Program." Paper presented at the Meeting of the Society for Research in Child Development, Tampa, Florida.

Schweinhart, L. And D. Weikart. (1993), "Success by Empowerment: the High Scope/Perry Preschool Study through Age 27." *Young Children.*

SII Taskforce (forthcoming) Impact Investment: The Invisible Heart of Markets, September 2014.

United Nations Office on Drugs and Crimes UNDOC (2011) Crime Series: www.unodc.org. In OECD (2014), *Society at a Glance*, OECD Publishing, Paris.

Chapter 5

Social impact investment market data: Initial findings

This chapter summarises the initial work on data collection, focusing on the G7 countries and Australia. It reviews the available data and current data collection processes and highlights some of the data challenges, including in terms of pulling together reliable and internationally comparable data. It also provides recommendations for moving forward.

5.1. Introduction

As seen in the development of other parts of capital markets (venture capital, angel investment, etc.) data on activity and performance can play an important role in helping to grow the market. Even at this early stage of development of the social impact investment market, a stronger evidence base would help in encouraging a global market to develop (HM Government, 2013c). Different players involved in the market, including policymakers, have been calling for more data on SII as well as a better and more accurate understanding of the size, scope, evolution and potential of the market.

A number of data challenges are common to all the parts of the SII framework. First, data needs to be collected in a more comparable way across countries. Harmonised definitions of social enterprises, social impact investors and social impact investment transactions are needed to facilitate cross country data collection efforts. Second, with unclear definitional boundaries, deciding what exactly is being measured (target population) is a major challenge and limits the scope for any sampling exercise. Third, and also as a result of definitional challenges, measurement errors are common, either overstating or understating the target population. Finally, it is unclear how detailed the data breakdown should be. Higher levels of granularity are more informative, but require data collection efforts that are more resource intensive and involve further related challenges in terms of deciding what should or should not be included as SII. Overcoming such barriers can help unlocking data that is not yet accessible.

This section discusses different data types, reviews which data are currently available, what types of data collection processes are currently in place and what other data is needed.[1]

5.2. Data types and data collection purposes

Before engaging in data collection it is important to clarify the goal of collecting the data. Policymakers might be interested in collecting data to monitor market developments, forecast future developments or evaluate policy interventions. Such data will necessarily need to include information on social needs and social outcomes. These objectives are different from those of other market participants that might want to collect data, for example, to inform investors of investment opportunities. In this case, relevant data will include current risk-return profiles, benchmarking, and forecasting potential market (and segment) growth, *inter alia*. Some players (mostly intermediaries) collect data as part of their business model, as it will be discussed later.

Different data types serve these different purposes. For example, while monitoring the market essentially requires data on SII transactions (deals and volumes), forecasting will need a good understanding of potential demand and supply. In doing so, we make a clear distinction between potential demand and supply on the one hand, and effective demand and supply and transactions (i.e. satisfied demand) on the other hand.

For example, looking at the demand-side for SII (a parallel can be drawn to the supply-side), potential demand for SII originates from unmet social needs (discussed in Chapter 4) and is translated into the SII market through delivery organisations that require funding to address such needs. Most currently available data on SII demand concerns potential demand (see Section 5.3). In other words, it measures a population of social delivery organisations that could potentially be SII investees. However, it is important to note that not all social delivery organisations will become investees. This will depend on their financing needs and funding preferences as discussed in Chapter 2. Legal structures are also important as they may inhibit some SII-type of funding (e.g. NPIs). Therefore, only a fraction of the social enterprise sector, for example, will be SII investees.

Second, it should be clear that identifying the potential demand for SII is different from measuring effective demand for SII. Some reports (e.g. NAB reports; Brown and Swersky, 2012) focus on identifying the scope for future SII demand, which contrasts for example with the information coming from surveys that aims at identifying financing needs within delivery organisations (see Section 6.3).

Third, satisfied demand is the effective demand that is matched by capital providers/investors (possibly through intermediaries) and results in SII transactions, including deals and flows.[2] The nature and sources of data that allow identifying the scope of potential and/or effective demand/supply, as well as transactions is likely to be different. For example, while transaction data will mainly come from intermediaries, estimating potential demand will require, *inter alia*, a combination of governmental data and detailed financial information on delivery organisations. Therefore, it is very important to decide *a priori* what type of data is needed to serve the purpose of a specific data collection effort.

5.3. Review of existing data sources: Data sources by framework component

Overall, current data availability on SII is very limited. A comprehensive picture of the SII market requires sizing the different components as discussed in Chapter 2: i) SII demand (including social needs and social service providers); ii) SII supply (i.e. pools of capital and investors); iii) SII intermediaries and financing instruments.

Annex 5.1 provides a list of SII data sources for G7 countries and Australia. The United Kingdom is the country in which most data is available, as a result of ten-year track record of SII market building, as well as a series of commissioned surveys and research papers. The list contains information gathered through desk research and further information received from participants in the Social Impact Investment Expert meetings. The data sources are organised in accordance to the SII framework. Three main data categories are identified and correspond to information on the demand (SII investees), supply (SI investors) and transactions (SII intermediaries). For each category, examples and some of the specific data challenges are described below.

5.3.1. Demand- side data

Demand-side data for SII includes information – both demographics and financial information – about a number of different market players that deliver social services or goods and are potential (or effective) investees. Table 5.1 below summarises the key demand-side players, data-related challenges as well as some examples of data sources. Demand side data can be obtained from different types of data sources.

Table 5.1. **Summary of type of demand-side players, challenges and data sources**

Organisation type	Definition and data challenges	Types of data sources
Social entrepreneurs (SE) Charities Non-profits institutions (NPIs) Social purpose organisations (SPOs) Cooperatives Development trusts Mutuals	No consensus on the type of organisation to be considered within the scope of SII Taxonomy is country-specific *"Solidarity" companies, FRA* Legal form of companies varies by country No match between legal form and the SI investee	Business registers/statistical offices (legal structure): *Community interest Companies (CIC), United Kingdom* Surveys: *SESS, CAN; ICSI2007, ITA* Certification organisations: *B-Corporation; IRIS; GIIRS* Associations: *Cooperative Association, GER* Directories: *Groupe SOS, FRA; Non-Profit Finance Fund, US;*

Note: Some examples are provided in italic below each point.

Source: OECD, based on desk research.

Some SII demand-side organisations have a specific legal structure or a generally accepted classification (e.g. community interest companies in the

United Kingdom, "entreprise solidaire" in France). It is possible to collect SII demand data, based on aggregation of data from organisations with specific legal form(s). The underlying information can be obtained from National Statistical Offices (NSOs) or other agencies that compile business register data. However, social enterprises and other social providers are defined by their objective of providing social outcomes, thus organised in many different legal forms (GHK, 2013). By providing incentives for social enterprises to report information (e.g. certification, visibility and investor networks), some organisations have been able to collect information on SII demand (e.g. B-Corporation, GIIRS).

Legal structures and certification do not always allow a precise mapping of SII demand-side organisations, nor do they necessarily provide financial data (important to understand financing needs). Creating a common and well defined legal type category for social businesses can help in identifying social companies and sizing the market as well as targeting policy. While in some countries, legal mechanisms that recognise some form of SII-related business structures are already in place, further efforts to create the appropriate formal enterprise structures are needed (WGMA, 2014).

An alternative to drawing upon legal form is to conduct demand side surveys, specially designed to identify the scope for SII demand. Surveys are the most common form of obtaining SII data and are discussed at length later in the chapter. The Non-profit Finance Fund survey in the United States is an example of a demand-side survey specifically aimed at understanding the financing needs of social enterprises. This was also the approach followed by the provincial-level Social Enterprise Sector Surveys initiative (SESS) in Canada described in Box 5.1. Close collaboration with local institutions and organisations was important to ensure a good coverage of the survey. The major drawback is that mapping SII using this approach can be extremely time consuming and resource intensive.

Box 5.1. **Social Enterprise Sector Survey**

Purpose

The Social Enterprise Sector Surveys (SESSs) are conducted within a project that aims at highlighting "the size, scope and impact of social enterprises at a provincial level". Identifying the demand for SII is not the original purpose of these surveys. However, by mapping the social enterprise sector along with the financial performance of identified social enterprises, SESSs can provide an indication of the scope for SII in the surveyed Canadian provinces. The first surveys were launched in 2010 (British Columbia and Alberta) and by the end of 2014, most Canadian provinces will have been covered at least by one survey wave. A total of 15 SESSs have either been completed or are currently being carried out.

Box 5.1. **Social Enterprise Sector Survey (cont.)**

Definition of social enterprise and survey approach

In order to conduct the surveys, a social enterprise (SE) were defined as follows:
In terms of function, the enterprise should "provide goods and services in the marketplace, motivated by a clear social, cultural, environmental or employment mission".

In terms of legal structure, the enterprise should i) be incorporated as a NPI or ii) be a private company 100% owned by a NPI.

This definition excludes a number of important organisations active in the SII market such as co-operatives, voluntary associations and, most importantly, social purpose business ventures and other forms of social business activity by the private sector. Therefore, this approach results in conservative estimates of the scope of the SE sector.

The objective is to survey the population of social enterprises in each Province, using the following steps:

identify potential social enterprises through a close collaboration with local institutions and organisations, knowledgeable about the potential scope of the SE sector in each province

contact potential social enterprises to screen out those that would not be considered as SE according to the working definition

send the questionnaire to identified SE.

Sampling challenges remain, in particular since it is not fully clear what is the representativeness of the sample. In addition, of those organisations identified as social enterprises, the response rate has, so far, been around 30-40% and obtaining further information on non-respondents still remains a challenge. Nevertheless, the strength of this approach is to focus on the local level and engaging with local organisations and institutions involved in the social enterprise sector, which allows for a better understanding of the potential scope of the sector in each region.

Resulting indicators

Indicators developed include business demographics, sales and revenue, expenditures, employment and volunteer engagement. These provide a broad overview of the scope of the SE sector as well as key characteristics of social enterprises across the different Provinces. More importantly, they contain information on the financial performance of social enterprises.

In addition to objective information on financial performance from expenditures and sales (and other forms of revenues), the new wave of surveys launched in 2014 also includes a number of questions regarding social enterprises' access to finance. As an example, the 2014 SESS for Alberta explicitly asks whether access to loans, access to grants or cash-flow management were a significant challenge for social enterprises. Together with objective financial information, survey results can provide a baseline estimate for the scope for SII in each Province.

Sources: Elson and Hall (2013); www.sess.ca/english/.

In addition, some types of social ventures belong to various associations and networks. This is, for example, the case of the Cooperative Association in Germany. The existence of such associations can help with sampling. Moreover, associations of specific types of delivery organisations (e.g. cooperatives) may also collect data on members. It is often in the interest of associations to disclose some information about their members for promotion purposes. Some organisations involved in SII activity also maintain directories of delivery organisations. This is, for example, the case of some NPIs active in SII such as the Groupe SOS in France, or financial intermediaries that share a list of its portfolio companies (e.g. Oltreventure; ClearlySo).[3] These associations and networks can be a key interlocutor in future data collection efforts.

Analysing the demand side of the SII framework involves a number of challenges. First, it is not yet clear what type of organisation should be considered within the scope of SII. For example the discussions are still evolving in terms of what exactly can be considered a social enterprise. Literature shows that social enterprise definitions have changed across time and geographies (Kerlin, 2010), and is strongly influenced by differences in social context. As an example, in the analysis of the 2013 Alberta SESS above, Elson et al. (2013) note that the definition of social enterprises "excludes social purpose business ventures and other forms of socially responsible business activity by the private sector, as well as enterprising activities by all orders of government". Changing definitions over time result in challenges for data interpretation. Focusing on the social intent of organisations, as described in Section 4, could help in identifying the demand side of the SII framework. However, collecting data based on social intent would require an objective and consensual measurement of intent.

Teasdale et al (2013) show how different criteria to identify social enterprises in the United Kingdom, used in surveys over time, has resulted in biased estimates of the growth of the social enterprise sector (Table 5.2). While for example initial surveys such as the ECOTEC, 2003 could understate the full extent of the social enterprise population (Type I error), the ASBS dataset compiled in 2007 might have included companies that are beyond the scope of the social enterprise concept (Type II error) – Type I and Type II errors are discussed at length in Section 5.4. Therefore, any interpretation of the increase from around 5 300 social enterprises in 2003 to around 60 000 in 2007 must take into account changing criteria over time.

Second, legal forms do not match what could be understood as an SII investee. Even if they did, these would not necessarily be comparable across countries. Due to the different systems, taxonomy varies from country to country. As an example, "solidarity" companies in France are not directly comparable to social cooperatives in Italy or community interest companies in the United Kingdom. In mapping the social enterprise sector across EU countries, Wilkinson et al. (2014) finds a wide range of legal forms and classifications in different countries.

Table 5.2. **Social enterprise in UK surveys**

Survey undertaken	Data source	Sampling Frame	Interpretation of key elements			Estimated social enterprise population
			a business	*primarily social objectives*	*reinvestment of surplus*	
1999–2003	ECOTEC, 2003	Existing local surveys	50% of income derived from trading	Governance and ownership structure based on democratic participation	Surplus can only be distributed to stakeholders as profit sharing or used for the benefit of the community	'up to 5,300'
2004	IFF Research, 2005	Companies Limited by Guarantee and Industrial and Provident Societies	25% of income derived through trading	The primary purpose is to pursue a social goal (or) to make profit for owners, partners and shareholders?	Asked whether profit is mainly distributed between owners, partners and shareholders; (or) mainly reinvested in the organisation or community, to further social goals?	'around 15,000'
2005	ASBS dataset 2005	All enterprises with less than 250 employees	25% of income derived through trading	Asks if organisation is a close fit with the DTI definition	organisations which do not pay more than 50% of profit to owners/shareholders	55,000
2007	ASBS dataset 2007	All enterprises with less than 250 employees	25% of income derived through trading	Asks if organisation is a close fit with the DTI definition	organisations which do not pay more than 50% of profit to owners/shareholders	70,000 (62,000 figure based on rolling average)
2009/10	NSTSO dataset 2010	Third sector organisations	50% of income derived through trading	Asks if organisation is a close fit with the DTI definition	Asks whether (all) surpluses are used to further social and/or environmental aims	8,507

Note: DTI stands for Department for Trade and Industry. In 2002 DTI defined social enterprise as "a business with primarily social objectives, whose surpluses are principally reinvested for that purpose in the business or in the community, rather than being driven by the need to maximise profit for shareholders and owners" (DTI, 2002). ASBS stands for the Annual Small Business Surveys where questions were added by DTI in order to assess the percentage of social enterprises in mainstream businesses. NSTSO is the National Survey of Third Sector Organisations. Please also refer to ECOTEC (2003) and ITF (2005).

Source: Teasdale et al. (2013).

Third, most of the information available on the demand side provides general demographic information on organisations that may require SII funding, but information on actual financing needs is scarce. Social enterprises do not necessarily disclose the relevant financial information needed to understand whether pressing financing needs exist. Therefore, information available is usually limited to a sample of firms for which financial information is available (e.g. Unicredit Foundation, 2012) or based on surveys that specifically ask for financing needs. In order to derive effective SII demand, it is necessary to look at how much financing delivery organisations need. Further efforts to collect data on financing constraints of social enterprises or information that allows for the estimation of the underlying financing needs (e.g. detailed financial information on social enterprises) are still needed.

5.3.2. Supply-side data

While not much data is available on effective supply of SII financing, except that obtained from surveys, investor platforms and transaction data sources, different data sources exist that provide information on potential pools of capital that could be deployed – Section 6.2 discusses the distinction between data on potential and effective SII activity. Also, SII supply forecasting exercises are increasingly common, but require strong assumptions such as the percentage of assets that may be committed to SII. As mentioned before, sources of data that allow measuring effective supply are likely to be different from those used for potential supply and forecasting.

Some data sources provide information on social impact investors and, more broadly, organisations providing finance to social ventures. As discussed earlier, the supply of SII can include a wide variety of players from foundations and venture philanthropy funds to institutional investors and high net worth individuals (HNWI). Governments also play an important role. Traditionally, they have been the largest providers of funding to address social issues, either through cash transfers or direct provision of social goods or services (see Chapter 5).

Table 5.3 below summarises the key supply-side players, data-related challenges as well as some examples of data sources. Supply-side data can be obtained from different types of data sources. Data related to the role of the government as a social impact investor can be obtained from NSOs. However, different levels of administration (central; regional; local) can entail measurement challenges. In countries in which some tax breaks may apply, for example in the United Kingdom, National Tax Offices will store information about eligible companies.[4] Also, in the United States, the IRS discloses a list of all organisations eligible to obtain tax-deductible charitable contributions.[5] Other institutions in the public sphere, such as central banks, financial market regulators and other financial supervisory bodies, monitor and compile information on investment activity and capital pools. The information is usually too aggregate, but can still be useful to estimate the potential capital that could be deployed into SII on the basis of a top-down approach due to difficulties in tracing-down actual SII amounts (Addis et al., 2013).

Associations and networks also track some data on investors. Examples of these include the Japan Foundation Centre for foundations; ACRI for bank foundations in Italy or EVPA for venture philanthropists across Europe. However, they typically only provide information on specific types of investors and coverage is limited to membership and to certain categories of data that fall short of what is needed for an effective mapping of SII.

Table 5.3. **Summary of type of supply-side players, challenges and data sources**

Organisation type	Definition and data challenges	Types of data sources
Government (national and local) Foundations Social venture funds Venture philanthropy funds Institutional investors Corporations High net worth individuals (HNWIs) Mass retail (crowdfunding) Untapped pools of capital (dormant funds)	Most information is on potential assets to be deployed The actual amount of SII is hard to trace. Sizing and assessing potential entails significant assumptions. Confidentiality issues	National statistical offices: *Social expenditures, National Accounts* Networks/associations: *Japan Foundation Center; EVPA, Europe* Surveys: *JP Morgan/GIIN;* National tax offices: *Tax breaks* Financial systems: *Financial Market Authorities; Central Banks*

Note: Some examples are provided in italic below each point.

Source: OECD, based on desk research.

Information about institutional investors sourced from the financial system (central banks and financial market authorities) as well as international organisations (e.g. OECD, IMF) and associations can also provide an indication of the size of assets that could potentially be deployed into SII, assuming a small percentage of those investors might be interested in SII. That interest would be conditional on a number of factors such as monetising social returns and the creation of adequate financial vehicles to attract investments from these investor types. A report by the World Economic Forum notes that these mainstream investors require at least a market risk adjusted financial return due to fiduciary responsibilities (WEF, 2013). The Asset Allocation Working Group report (WGAA, 2014) analyses how the fiduciary duty perception that SII cannot deliver required financial returns (amongst other challenges) has been limiting the allocation of funds to SII financial instruments. It also discusses how this challenge can be tackled and SII integrated into portfolio structures of mainstream investors in the future, increasing the opportunity for portfolio diversification.

Figure 5.1 below overviews financial assets held by major types of institutional investors for G7 and Australia. In comparison to GDP, these institutional investors hold large sums of money, even though investments may often take place overseas. In some cases representing more than 90% of GDP (e.g. pension funds in the United Kingdom and insurance companies in France), institutional investors can steer the SII market even if committing extremely small shares of their total portfolios into SII.

Figure 5.1. **Financial assets of institutional investors**

As a percentage of GDP, 2011

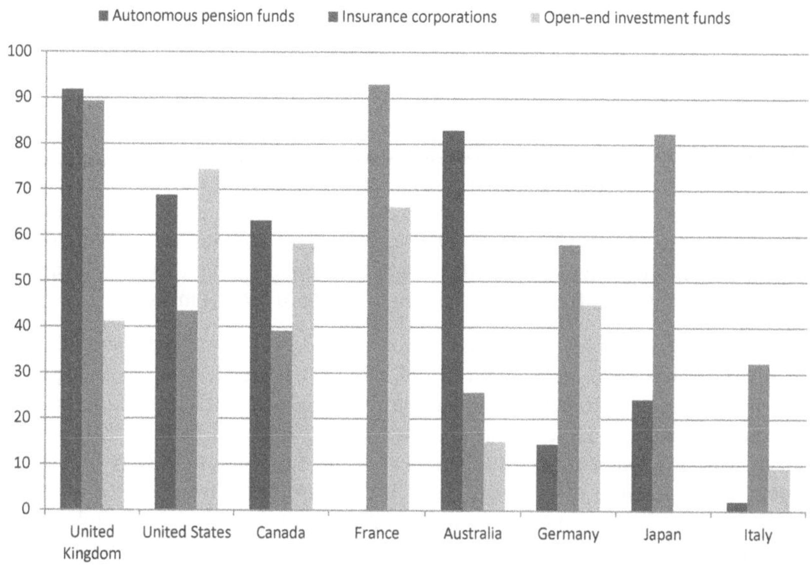

Source: OECD (2013f).

As in other areas, surveys have been the main tool to profile social impact investors and quantify available capital. For example, in the JP Morgan/ GIIN Impact Investor Survey series (Box 5.2 below) the survey sample has been increasing. This imposes some limits to a longitudinal analysis – in the last survey a subsample of respondents overlapping with the previous edition (67 out of 125) was used to make a comparative statics analysis. The most important is to guarantee that the sample provides a good idea about the effective distribution of characteristics across different investors.

The GIIN/JP Morgan survey is particularly interesting because it combines quantitative information (e.g. investments; assets under management; returns) with qualitative information (e.g. growth perspectives; return expectations). If efforts are made to obtain a representative sample with longitudinal data, it is possible to track if investors' expectations regarding the SII market are actually being met (e.g. Saltuk et al., 2014).

An important challenge in collecting supply-side data relates to confidentiality requirements. This is also an issue for data collection in the venture capital and angel investment markets, in which supply side data is collected by survey from investors. For example, while most information from financial system regulators is not disclosed, data originating from survey exercises often needs to be anonymised (e.g. if it requires the disclosure proprietary or other types of sensitive data). For example, confidentiality issues can be particularly relevant for high net-worth individual.

Box 5.2. **GIIN and JP Morgan survey**

J.P. Morgan and the GIIN have been collecting data on impact investors through surveys since 2011. The joint surveys target investing organisations such as foundations, funds or financial institutions and apply a broad definition of impact investment, as described in Chapter 4. Individual investors are however excluded from the analysis. Also, only investors with assets under management above USD 10 million are included. As a consequence, the resulting sample is not representative of the whole SII market. Nevertheless, it is amongst the most comprehensive sets of information on the supply side of the SII market.

So far, three different survey waves have been carried out (2011, 2012 and 2013) and the sample of investors has been increasing (52, 99 and 125, respectively). Also, respondents do not necessarily overlap which means that caution is needed when interpreting trends along the different survey waves. The table below provides a comparison of targeted SII (amounts that investors are willing to invest) and the actual investment volumes in 2011, 2012 and 2013 survey waves. It is possible to see significant investment leaps between the survey waves. These cannot be regarded as market growth but rather sampling changes. Saltuk et al. (2014) make a comparative analysis that carefully focuses on the 67 survey respondents that had participated the year before (Saltuk, 2013). Tracking the exact same individuals would allow comparing *a priori* targeted investments for a given year with the subsequent volume of investments in that year.

2011 survey	2012 survey		2013 survey	
n=52	n=88	n=87 (2013)	n=125	n=124 (2014)
Targeted 2012	Transactions (volume) 2012	Targeted 2013	Transactions (volume) 2013	Targeted 2014
3.8 investments	8.0 investments	9.1 investments	10.6 investments	12.7 investments

Notes: in billion USD. Information on survey response rates is not available.

The survey results convey information on a number of different investor characteristics, including investor size (AUM), investor type (e.g. family office, fund manager, foundations, etc…), headquarters and geographical focus, sector focus, asset class focus, investment stage focus, return expectations, sources of capital (for intermediaries).

In addition, information is also gathered with respect to investors' perspectives, in particular regarding: i) adequate risk and return profiles; ii) motivations for impact investments; iii) evolution of the SII market (e.g. usage of standards, investment opportunities, availability of capital for SII); iv) major challenges for impact investing; v) role of policy; vi) planned investments in the near future (1 year); vii) importance of metrics to evaluate performance.

Source: Saltuk et al. (2011; 2013; 2014).

5.3.3. Intermediaries and transactions

In terms of sizing the SII market, obtaining transaction data is crucial. However, this type of data is very hard to access, perhaps due to the fact that the market is still in embryonic phase in most countries and the necessary data collection processes have not been put in place. Currently the data remains in small pockets, used only by those directly involved in the transactions.

Table 5.4 below summarises the key intermediaries, data-related challenges, as well as some examples of data sources. Data on intermediaries and transactions can be obtained from different types of data sources. Transaction data is collected by social banks and wholesale banks such as Big Society Capital in the United Kingdom. Social exchanges have recently been established in some G7 countries such as the United Kingdom (Social Stock Exchange) and Canada (SVX) although the earliest exchanges were developed in other countries. With increasing deal activity, these exchanges can become an important source of SII transaction data in the near future. Nevertheless, transactions through social stock exchanges will likely only account for a small share of total SII activity.

Table 5.4. **Summary of types of intermediaries, challenges and data sources**

Organisation type	Definition and data challenges	Types of data sources
Social banks Social investment wholesale banks Community development finance institutions (CDFIs) Fund managers and tax advantage funds Social exchanges Crowdfunding platforms SII Networks/platforms DFIs and development banks	Several organisations collecting data but different types and in various ways. Data usually collected to address investor needs. Market still in embryonic phase in most countries. Identifying the set of intermediaries can be helpful to identify all potential players collecting transaction data	Banks/wholesale banks: *BSC, UK; Bpifrance, France* Funds: *Impact Assets; NCIF, US;* Social exchanges: *Social Stock Exchange, UK; SVX, CAN* Investor platforms: *Impact Base, GIIN; Maximpact; Engaged Investment, UK* Crowdfunding platforms: *Masssolution, US* Networks/associations: *Finansol, FRA; CFDA, UK*

Note: Some examples are provided in italic below each point.

Source: OECD, based on desk research.

In parallel, the number of SII investor platforms has been increasing in recent years. These platforms provide a useful tool for investors interested in investing with a social impact. In addition, they gather information on investees, investors and, in some cases, transactions. Impact Base from GIIN or Maximpact (yet to become operational) are examples of platforms from which transaction data can be obtained. Some platforms, such as Engaged Investment in the United Kingdom, are not only collecting raw SII transaction data, but also developing taxonomy with the objective of constructing SII market indexes (see Box 5.3). In addition, there are specific types of platforms, such as Massolution in the United States, that gather information on certain types of transactions (in this example, crowdfunding), some of which might be classified as SII.

Tax can play an important role in the SII market (City of London, 2013). Information on special tax regimes exists for example in the United Kingdom for social impact investment (Social investment tax relief). Tax offices would, in theory, be able to gather and aggregate such information, based on any tax credits and tax rebates that may apply. This approach could potentially provide a more comprehensive overview of both the number and volume of SII deals. However, accessing such administrative data is not always possible and requires overcoming confidentiality issues.

Even though data from some of these venture capital associations or angel investor networks can be fairly comprehensive, usually it only covers information obtained from members or associates. This caveat is even more important in areas where the association/network might only represent a small share of the market players. This is, for example, the case of business angel associations and networks. The case with SII is even more challenging given the varying views on definitions and the potential incentives for investors to classify themselves as social impact investors when they might not qualify. Rapidly growing SII-related associations such as Venture Philanthropy Associations (e.g. EVPA in Europe or AVPN in Asia) will certainly be important in future data collection efforts.

The main challenge in sourcing data from intermediaries is that it is usually collected to address investor needs. Data disaggregation, in terms of social areas, relevant to a policymaker might be very different from the breakout and labels that would be appealing to an investor. It is important to distinguish the data requirements of investors, researchers and policymakers as outlined in Section 6.2. For example, while data collected for investors should reflect mostly financial characteristics (e.g. risk-return profiles, investor perspectives and investor practices, track record), data for policymakers should make the link with social outcomes and collected in such a way to provide the basis for informed policy action. Further work is needed to obtain data in a way that can provide insights for policy guidance.

Box 5.3. **Benchmarking SII: EngagedX**

EngagedX collects SII transaction data with the objective of aggregating it into time-series market data that can be used to benchmark the performance of individual investments, funds or capital managers. Anonymised transaction data is being shared by leading SII intermediaries and fund managers in the United Kingdom, with plans to scale globally. EngagedX has been commissioned by the Social Investment Research Council (comprising Big Lottery Fund, Big Society Capital, the Cabinet Office, Citi and The City of London Corporation) to assemble a dataset of historic performance of the UK market. This dataset will bring together comparative data about outturn risk and returns of investments in relation to capital pricing.

Data is collected and normalised according to a reporting framework developed collaboratively by EngagedX and industry practitioners. This helps categorise and compare transactions according to a number of characteristics, including product type, risk banding, sectors, investor and investee characteristics as well as the nature of social outcomes. The figure below depicts the high level architecture of the EngagedX data model.

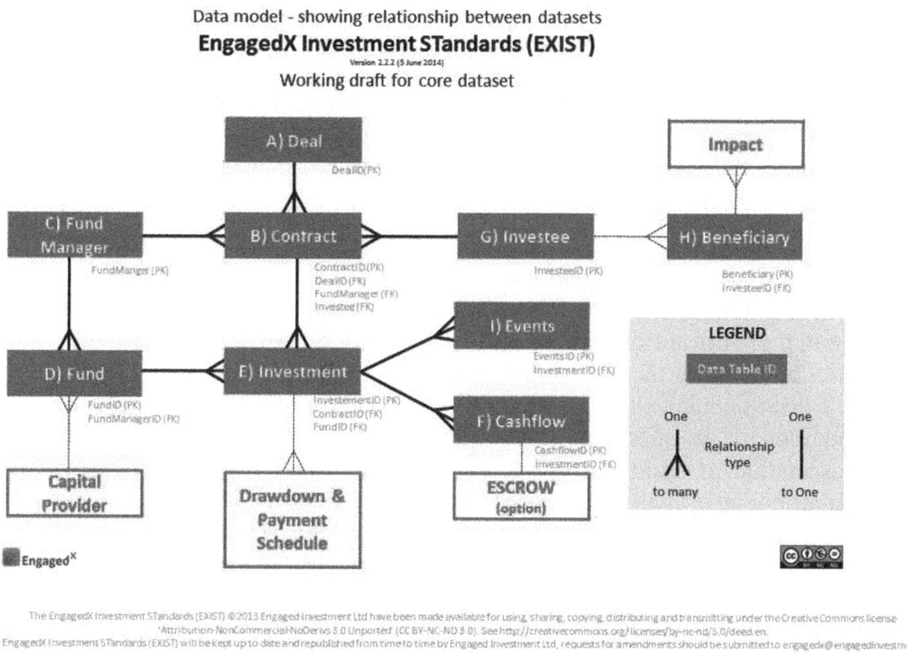

Source: EngagedX Investment STandards (EXIST), Version 2.2.2 (5 June 2014).

The resulting information will help showcase the risk-return profiles of SII in relation to mainstream capital markets. It will also identify the different drivers of social and financial performance in SII as well as how risk-return benchmarks vary across different social areas, geography or other relevant market segmentation.

Source: www.engagedinvestment.com (accessed 18 July 2014).

5.4. Current approaches to data collection

Various approaches might be used to collect SII information depending on which parts of the market are being assessed. However, none of the currently available approaches are optimal. The first is a top-down approach where key national aggregates are identified that allow the estimation of the SII market conditional on (strong) assumptions. The second is to compile information from players that have a common legal form directly linked to SII. The third is to collect data via surveys from market actors. Data requirements can also vary depending on who is seeking the data (market players, academics, policy makers). The details, advantages and disadvantages of each approach are described below.

5.4.1. Top-down approach

Some of the components of the SII framework can be estimated using a top-down approach. Within this approach, the first step is to obtain data on national aggregates. Since this data are highly aggregated, it combines a myriad of different information sets that go beyond SII. Therefore, the key is to single out the SII components. For this exercise a number of (rather strong) assumptions are required. First, it requires that some (rough) idea of the shares of the SII component, which needs to be based either on perceptions or historical information.

While using shares based on perceptions can be misleading, depending on historical data assumes that it is: i) representative of the SII market; and, ii) there are no structural shifts, and thus percentages remain the same. On one hand, significant challenges still remain in terms of sizing the market. On the other hand, the SII market is evolving and growing rapidly, which means that assuming stable shares of the SII component might be unrealistic. In addition, it is important to note that even if shares provide a good representation of reality in one country, it will likely not be the case in different countries with different social systems. As a result, this approach has significant limitations. Although it can be useful to provide rough estimates of the market and foresights of demand and supply in the coming years, it does not allow effective measurement of SII demand or supply, nor is it able to provide insights into SII deal flows.

Examples of the use of this approach can be found in measurement exercises focusing on potential funding from institutional investors or funding from governments. As an example, work being carried out by NABs has provided information on the scope of public expenditures and public procurement based on National Accounts aggregates. The potential SII demand was identified by narrowing down to social service delivery funded by government. Another potential use of this approach is the measurement of potential investments by institutional investors as described in section 5.3.2.

5.4.2. Bottom-up approach

A different approach to sizing SII components is to focus on individual units (e.g. social enterprises, specific types of investors or intermediaries). This approach requires that sufficiently detailed information is available at a high level of disaggregation that allows identifying individual units within SII. Information to identify SII delivery organisations would include sector of economic activity, legal form, business description/mission, *inter alia.* This information could either come from NSO micro databases or from commercial data providers. As a second step, it is then essential to understand whether the individual units gathered represent the population or a subset of it. In the most likely case that it only represents a subset of the population, it is important to ensure that the sample is representative (e.g. through observing characteristics contained in the data). Finally, based on the information gathered, the SII component can be measured either through aggregation (if the population is observed) or by inference (if using a subset of the population).

Box 5.4. **Satellite Account on Non-Profit Institutions**

The Satellite Account on Non-Profit Institutions (NPIs) was introduced to respond to a growing non-profit sector that was not taken into account in the agreed System of National Accounts (SNA 1993). The Handbook (UN, 2003) provides guidance regarding the identification of all NPIs, in particular through a clear definition of NPI, the valuation of volunteer work and by introducing a classification system for NPIs based on their function. The need for improved data coverage – insofar as there were no incentives for NSOs to collect data on NPIs – and the increased policy relevance, were also key motives for developing this system.

There are a number of distinctive characteristics in NPIs that required a specific statistical approach, different than the applied to corporations and governmental units. Some of these characteristics, such as the revenue structure, capital sources or tax treatment, can also be found in SII. By classifying NPIs into 12 group types (see Table A.6.1, Annex) and providing a system for categorising revenues and expenses as well as volunteer work, donations, as well as *non-market output*, the Satellite Account for NPIs provides a harmonised framework for mapping the NPI sector. Also, it provides data on the extent to which foundations fund other parts of the non-profit sector such as health or research

For the case of SII, it would be important to highlight the measurement of *non-market output*. While the traditional SNA measures output through sales revenue. For the case of some NPIs and SII, part of the output will not be measured this way and output will be undervalued. This is particularly the case if an organisation has a significant portion of its revenue coming from donations and other non-sales types of revenue. The measurement approach does not attempt to value non-market output. Instead, the valuation of non-market output is based on the difference between costs and sales. If negative the non-market output will be zero, if positive it will be equal to the difference between sales and costs. Even though this approach is not optimal, it provides a practical solution to the measurement issue.

Source: UN (2003).

The key challenge of using this approach is ensuring that either the whole population is observed or the sample is representative. Section 5.6 discusses sampling challenges at length. The emphasis given to NSOs derives from the fact that they usually provide information on a population set or at least on a representative sample. In addition NSOs have expertise in collection of high quality data in a consistent, cross country comparable way. The United Nations Handbook on Non-Profit Institutions in the System of National Accounts (UN, 2003) provides guidance for NSOs to identify and collect data on NPIs. An interesting feature is the practical solution to the measurement approach to non-market output (i.e. social impact). As a long term goal, it would be important to consider agreement on definitions and legal structures in such a way that (demand) data can be collected in a systematic and internationally comparable way by NSOs.

Examples of this approach can be found in efforts to size the demand side of the SII framework (specifically measuring the social enterprise sector). In a study of the Italian social enterprise sector, Fedele and Miniaci (2010) use commercial data sources (Amadeus database from Bureau van Dijk) to distinguish the capital structure of cooperatives (proxy for social companies) *vis a vis* for profit enterprises.

5.4.3. Surveys

The most direct source of data is to conduct surveys of key actors in the market. Surveys can be very resource-intensive, but provide extremely rich information if well designed and implemented. The first step in a survey process is to identify key SII players – social enterprises, investors or intermediaries, depending on the SII component under analysis. This is challenging, since depending on the type of survey respondent, greater detail and data granularity can be achieved.

Recently, the OECD carried out a survey of Social Economy Organisations (SEOs), understood as organisations with non-profit objectives, operating in 14 different regions, corresponding to 8 countries (OECD 2013g). The geographical scope was limited, but the results insightful. The survey was answered by 655 SEOs and revealed that, on average, SEOs finance themselves mostly through internal resources – i.e. their "profit"/cash generating ability – (31.8%) and subsidies (30.6%). In addition, as the level of detail increases, so do survey costs.[6]

Second, survey design is crucial for efficiently and effectively achieving the objectives of the analysis. In designing surveys, it is important to reach the right balance between the amount of information requested and simplicity – i.e. respondents may feel less encouraged to complete the survey if it becomes too complex and time consuming. Also it is important to consider sampling frames to be able to know what part of the population is being surveyed (ensure representativeness). To date, most surveys on SII have focused on selected networks of key market players in certain geographies and therefore it is not clear whether the data is representative of the population.

Survey response rates are often lower than initially expected. It is important to understand why there are non-respondents. Designing the appropriate incentives for reporting good quality data is essential. Moral hazard issues in previous data collection efforts were identified during the OECD SII Expert Meeting in Paris. Incentives should ensure that, for example, portfolio losses are reported in a rigorous way. In addition, it is important to note that incentives should be tailored to the type of SII player being surveyed. For example, showing respondents part of the survey outcomes could provide a good incentive to some types of respondents such as fund managers.

Third, data control and verification mechanisms are crucial to ensure high data quality standards. In some surveys carried thus far, data was checked through registration documents (e.g. Saltuk et al., 2011, 2013, 2014). Finally, building upon the sample collected while ensuring its representativeness, it is possible to draw broader conclusions about SII activity (inference making).

The CASE initiative on impact investing (CASE i3) provides good examples of surveys aimed at building the SII evidence base. Launched in 2010 it partners with different market players (social entrepreneurs, investors, academics and policymakers) in order to provide build the SII evidence base (Box 5.5). An interesting feature of this initiative is the simultaneous focus on the demand and supply sides of SII.

Since the beginning, CASE i3 has been collecting data via surveys on social entrepreneurs and impact funds, in collaboration with B-Corporation and GIIRS, respectively. The survey of demand side organisations is used to label companies as a B-corp (Box 5.6). Therefore, there is a high incentive for companies to report the data because they can benefit from the label. The survey has been being improved over time (will soon be in its third version) and efforts have been made to reduce the number of questions (above 100). Since the main goal is to profile companies, financial information is very scarce (only includes one variable on total revenue), which would be important for the purposes of estimating SII demand. Also, the focus is on for-profit organisations, so, again, it might not fully cover what is understood as SII (e.g. including NPIs; Cooperatives). CASE i3 has also commissioned research in 2012 to investigate the benefits of being labelled as a B-corp (this research is still ongoing). With this respect, the challenge is to have an unbiased and representative sample of B-corps and non-B-corps so that robust comparisons can be made.

Box 5.5. **CASE i3 work on building the evidence base**

Case is a recent initiative launched in 2010 by the Center for the Advancement of Social Entrepreneurship (CASE), based at Duke University's Fuqua School of Business, United States.

Within CASE i3, a number of surveys have been carried out, either focusing on social entrepreneurs or on investors. The surveys are done in partnership with B Lab (focusing on social entrepreneurship) and with GIIRS (aimed at impact investment funds). Two separate datasets on companies and impact funds are maintained by CASEi3. As of March 2013, the company dataset covered over 8 000 for-profit impact entrepreneurs. In terms of the funds database, it covers a total of over USD 4.5Bn in AUM.

CASE i3 also runs a MBA on Impact Investing. This is an interesting approach that accrues benefits in terms of increased research capacity, since students are involved in consultancy and research work, while engaging with academics and practitioners in the field of Impact Investing.

Case i3 also has the capacity to commission research to outside academics and consultants which further enriches the contribution of the initiative to advancing the knowledge about the SII empirical base. In particular, it commissioned research in 2012 to work with the data collected on social entrepreneurs with the objectives of i) making comparative analysis of the effects of being a B-corporation and ii) improving the data collection mechanism (including streamlining the survey). A new call for research proposals is expected for September 2014 and will focus on analysing the supply side data. A sample of the survey can be found online.

The data on funds has been used for a report (Clark et al., 2013), in which 12 funds were selected from 30 very successful Impact funds (out of an initial list of 350 potential impact funds) and analysed in detail. These selected funds accounted for USD 1.3bn total assets.

Data collected includes proprietary information so it is only disclosed to the greater public at aggregated levels through a series of reports and working papers. Nevertheless B-corp profile information is made available and includes company general information and

Source: CASE i3 website at http://sites.duke.edu/casei3/.

The survey on the supply side provides information on fund performance that can then be linked to portfolio company data. The objective is to provide input for the GIIRS rating system that rates both funds and portfolio companies. The ratings do not result from financial performance but rather focus on the (potential) for social/environmental impact. The underlying survey and quality check procedures used in GIIRS follow the same structure as those used for B-corp but the survey questions and type of information requested is adapted to serve the rating purposes. The data reporting burden is shared between the fund and portfolio companies as both benefit from being rated.

Surveys are extremely resource intensive and entail significant challenges in terms of identifying appropriate samples. Population and sampling issues are discussed at length in Section 5.6. Developing a resource-efficient way to exhaustively map the SII market remains a challenge.

Scoping exercises and pilot surveys can provide valuable input to improving SII survey design. However, new survey initiatives should be made in collaboration with existing efforts, to build upon existing experience as well as avoid survey fatigue. This is particularly relevant at early stages of market development, when different organisations may end up collecting data simultaneously. To collect globally, cross-country comparable data, new survey instruments may be needed, but should be implemented in partnership with existing initiatives and provide a broader coverage of SII activity across countries.

Different data approaches might be more appropriate to size different parts of the SII market given its current embryonic state. For the demand side, bottom-up approaches that rely on some form of SII-related legal form or classification might be preferable; however, for investors a top-down approach could be sufficiently informative. However, surveys appear to be the best overall option at the moment – despite high costs, sampling issues and survey fatigue risks – since not much information on SII is available.

5.5. Current SII data and market estimation

The SII market and concepts are new in most countries, thus the evidence base is very scarce. Market estimates mainly come from industry reports, while some academics have focused on measuring the scope of SII activity. This process has been facilitated by the work of the National Advisory Boards set up by the Social Impact Investment Taskforce established by the G8 and new initiatives such as Expert Group on Social Entrepreneurship in the European Union or the CASE i3 in the US have helped building the evidence base and pushing forward the data discussion.[7]

5.5.1. Academic literature building on SII data

Even though academic literature on social enterprises is large, academic literature on SII is relatively scarce. In particular, academic papers that attempt to measure the scope of SII are rare. Table 5.5 below provides examples of the academic literature that focus on gathering and analysis SII-related data.

In terms of market components, most of the advances in data analysis have been on the demand side. The academic literature on social enterprises is extensive. For example, international research networks specifically devoted to social enterprises (e.g. EMES; TEPSIE) have been established and contributed to advances in the understanding of the social enterprise sector.[8] Mapping of social enterprises (*lactu sensu*) exist for a number of countries. Smith and Rothbaum (2013) provide an overview of business demographics trends related co-operatives across several countries, including Canada, France, Germany, Italy, the United Kingdom and the United States.

Table 5.5. **Examples from academic literature**

Article	Country	Data	Source
Alcock et al (2012)	UK	Case study (SEIF)	Survey covering 1653 companies (285 treated+1368 non-treated)
Lyon et al (2010)	UK	Case study (SEIF)	Survey – see Alcock et al. (2012)
Nicholls (2010b)	UK	Rough UK landscape	Different reports
Nicholls (2010a)	Global (focus UK)	Broad mapping	N/A
Anttonen and Haikio (2011)	Finland	Demand indicators in elderly-care sector	Documents provided by Min. Social Affairs and Health
Hazenberg (2011)	UK	15 SIFIs (out of 22 identified)	Interviews with fund managers
Florek (2013)	UK	Community interest companies	National Survey of Third Sector Organisations
Mendel and Barbosa (2013)	Global	Exchange platforms	Exchange platforms websites
Blazy (2011)	FRA; USA	Sizing social sector. SII in USA	Government sources for FRA (e.g. DARES). Reports and Gvt sources for US (e.g. CDFI Fund)
Wells (2012)	UK	Case study (Futurebuilders)	FBE Annual Review Data
Borzaga et al (2010-WP)	ITA	sample of 320 Italian social cooperatives	ICSI2007 database; see also Scalvini et al (2007)
Fedele and Miniaci (2010-WP)	ITA	2007 balance sheet data for 504 companies, of which 226 are cooperatives (proxy for social companies)	Bureau van Dijk – Amadeus.
Smith and Rothbaum (2013)	Global	Cooperatives	Canada: Rural and Cooperatives Secretariat; France: Les Scop and INSEE Germany: DGRV; Geschäftsbericht Italy: Census on Cooperatives UK: Co-operatives UK; US: University of Wisconsin Center for Cooperatives

Source: OECD, based on desk research.

The academic literature is not very prolific in terms of studies analysing and mapping investors and intermediaries. While some papers go into detail on a specific market component (e.g. Mendel and Barbosa, 2013 overview existing exchange platforms), others focus on case studies of specific instruments (e.g. Alcock et al., 2012 evaluate the impact of the SEIF in the United Kingdom). Therefore, the mapping of SII is always very incomplete. Recent research initiatives such as the CASE i3, described before in Box 5.5, are aiming at providing robust evidence on the SII market as a whole.

5.5.2. Industry reports

While there are few academic papers, an increasing number of industry reports have attempted to size the SII market. These reports look at the market from different angles and often use different definitions that may include different things. Many of these reports focus on certain countries, geographies or sectors providing a window into parts of the SII market but a fragmented and sometimes contradictory view on the overall market. Without a comprehensive picture – either in terms of market potential, effective demand/supply or actual transactions – data collection efforts can result in significant biases.

A number of these reports build on the same few data sources and on limited evidence from case studies (and many of the same cases are used repeatedly). To date, most SII data obtained comes from surveys (e.g. Saltuk et al, 2011, 2013, 2014) and interviews that have been conducted by SII intermediaries, government agencies and/or consulting firms. Even though the information collected in these reports is a big step forward towards a better understanding of SII, sample sizes are often limited and estimates of the SII market often require strong assumptions.

A number of industry reports have provided some estimates on the actual (or potential) size of the SII market. Table 5.6 below provides examples of SII market estimates as well as a brief explanation of the approached followed. Few reports focus on actual transactions, rather measuring effective demand and (quite often) estimating the market potential and forecasting future market growth. These numbers should be regarded with caution since they rely on rather strong assumptions and the underlying market estimation effort entails a non-negligible number of challenges. The estimates presented in the table are just illustrative since the underlying data and methodologies are very different due to data availability in each country. Therefore, any comparison of estimates across reports should be avoided.

The strategies to collect data previously described can broadly be found in the existing industry estimates of the SII market. As an example, Weber and Scheck (2012) take a bottom-up approach to size the German SII market, by compiling information on a number of major SII investors. Specifically, they sum up the assets, investments and funding from BonVenture, the Social Venture Fund, Auridis GmbH and the KfW funding. Therefore the estimates might be downward biased since not all SII players are included due to data collection challenges.

Table 5.6. **Some market estimates from industry reports**

Report	Country/ region	Estimate/ MKT potential	Type	Approach	Estimate year
Brown and Norman (2011)	England	GBP 165 million	Potential	Survey (78 SIFIs)	2010/11
Brown and Swersky (2012)	England	GBP 750 million potential demand (£1 bn in 2016)	Potential	Mixed, but essentially Bottom-up (starting from sector level demand)	2015
Saltuk et al. (2014)	Global	USD 10.6 bn commitments	Effective and Transactions	Survey (125 investors)	2013
Addis et al.(2013)	AUS	AUD 300 million investment, AUD 2 billion AUM	Potential	Top-down	2012
Harji et al. (2014)	CAN	>CAD 1.6 bn in AUM	Effective and Transactions	Survey and interviews	2013
Chua et al. (2011)	Asia	USD 44-74 bn potential AUM	Potential	Bottom-up (starting from sector level demand)	2020
La Croix (2014)	FRA	EUR 6.02 bn Solidarity-based AUM	Effective and Transactions	Member reporting	2012
Clark et al. (2013)	Global	USD 1.3 bn total assets (12 funds)	Effective	Survey	2013
Weber and Scheck (2012)	GER	EUR 24 million market volume	Effective	Bottom up (Sum of key SII investors)	2012
Hope Consulting (2011)	USA	USD 120 bn (willingness to invest in high performing non-profits)	Potential	Survey (5 227 individuals; 873 investment advisors; 727 foundations)	2010
Freireich and Fulton (2009)	USA	USD 26 bn community investing	Transactions	N/A	2007

Notes: Estimate year refers to the date to which the estimate corresponds to (usually different from publication date). AUM stands for assets under management.

Source: OECD, based on desk research.

As discussed before, estimating the actual size of the market requires a different approach, as well as different data and respective sources. The strategy followed by Brown and Swersky (2012) to forecast future SII investment demand was the following. First, a number of key SII sectors were identified and further disaggregated into 26 subsectors. Second, the share of economic activity performed by social organisations was calculated for each subsector. Third, the capital requirements of social organisations were calculated by sector. Finally, by comparing present with future capital requirement (based on sector growth and capital depreciation assumptions), it is possible to calculate the investment needs and thus forecast future SII demand. The underlying raw data is obtained through a combination of a survey to 40 SII market players, interviews and publicly available data sources, in a mixed bottom-up (sector level) and survey approach.

The pure survey approach is followed by Saltuk et al. (2014) and is described in Box 5.2. As previously discussed, the key for successfully estimating the SII market is to guarantee that the sample is representative of the target population and that selection biases are mitigated. These remain key challenges in nearly all SII surveys because the boundaries of the target population (and definition) are still blurry.

A common caveat found in most industry reports relates to the strategies employed to estimate the current (or potential) market. Strong assumptions, such as constant shares (across time and geography) for the SII component of more aggregate measures can induce significant biases. Also, it is sometimes assumed a nexus/relationship between SII demand and supply that is not self-evident. For example, Chua et al. (2011) first calculate a sector-level SII demand projection assuming that 5% to 15% of total demand in each sector is satisfied through SII. Second, building on the demand estimate, the SII total invested capital is calculated through a formula based on estimated profit margins (by sector), return on equity and average cost of capital.

An additional caveat found in some industry reports is an emphasis on case studies and/or a selection of very successful SII transactions, investors or social enterprises (e.g. Clark et al., 2013). In particular if such small (and biased) samples are built upon to draw conclusions on the evolution of the SII market. It should be noted however, that such reports do not claim to size the whole SII market, but rather provide a kick-start to the discussion on building the evidence base. Avoiding selection biases is crucial and to do so, it is crucial to include in the samples not only the best and the good, but also the not so well performing cases (Bloom and Clark, 2011). The right incentives need to be devised in order to ensure the survey participation of, at least a representative sample of the target population. Providing feedback on interim survey results can be a good incentive to increase survey participation (Bloom and Clark, 2011).

5.6. Challenges in SII data collection

Scoping and sizing the global SII market is an enormous challenge. There is no consensual definition across different geographies and, above all, market players and researchers involved in SII. This implies that most market estimates are not directly comparable. Data is not being collected in a standardised and systematic way.

Most importantly, the lack of a consensual definition creates enormous challenges in identifying the target population – i.e. what exactly is being measured. For example, the scope of SII demand cannot possibly be identified as long as the boundaries of SII delivery organisations are blurry. Sampling schemes avoid the need to capture information about the whole population by focusing on a representative subset. However, sampling requires a clear definition of the population along with a number of key observable characteristics. So, in the case of SII, even if a sampling frame is properly devised and a robust sampling methodology is used, it results in biased estimates because it is unclear what the population of interest should be in the first place. In other words, it is not possible to find a subset of the populations that, according to some observable characteristics, is representative of the population. Therefore, estimates of SII scoping exercises are usually biased towards certain sectors, instruments or investor types. Accordingly, extrapolating total market sizes based on limited and unrepresentative samples should be regarded with caution. Chapter 3 of this report provides a structure that helps defining SII, the basis for engaging in data collection efforts.

In most measurement exercises, a common error is to exclude data that could be relevant (Type I error). In the case of SII, focusing on a narrower scope can result in significantly incorrect measurements. For example in Clark et al. (2013) only a selected number of intermediaries were analysed. The coverage in the series of GIIN/JP Morgan investor surveys (Saltuk et al., 2011; 2013; 2014) has been increasing, which reveals that some important investors might be (or have been) left out.

However, the early stage of SII market development can potentiate another type of measurement errors: including data that is not relevant for SII (Type II error). For example, applying the working definition described in Chapter 3, some delivery organisations can be wrongly included as SII investees. As discussed in that section of the paper, some certified B-corps may not be included in the potential demand for SII, because some of the certified companies would not meet the other necessary eligibility criteria for SII. Another example can be found in the ASSB dataset in the United Kingdom, which samples social enterprises from all existing firms with less than 250 employees (see Section 5.3).

The lack of a statistical definition of SII means that data is embedded in other broader data categories. Disentangling what is the subset of information that corresponds to SII can be extremely challenging. For example, in top-down approaches very strong assumptions are usually required, as discussed earlier in this section. In addition there are several SII data layers (e.g. social need granularity) which add substantial complexity to the analysis. A more granular approach may require data collection efforts that are more resource intensive and might entail additional confidentiality issues. The trade-off between level of detail and comprehensiveness of the information should be taken into account when deciding to collect data. As an example, for the purpose of analysing SII transactions, survey respondents might include investor platforms or the investors themselves. While focusing on investors provides a greater level of detail, it multiplies the number of respondents, thus increasing data treatment and survey management needs.

Finally, a common challenge in data collection is clarifying why, what and for whom data should be collected. This is particularly important because different goals require different data types (and data sources). Having a clear goal for data collection and well-defined data requirements is crucial. Two types of measurement objectives were identified in the OECD SII Expert Meeting in London. On the one hand, it is important to further understand the evolution and behaviour of the SII market to inform policymakers of any regulatory adjustments that might be needed. On the other hand, data collection efforts should also serve to inform investors about SII market potentiality.

Priority should be given to capturing objective data before stepping into areas where definitions are not yet established and data is deemed subjective. This may apply to either demand, supply or transaction data. However, given that transaction data usually entails some information on both demand and supply, a thorough collection of this type of data can be a valuable starting point. In early stages of market development surveys can be a valuable tool. However, these are resource intensive and entail significant challenges in terms on ensuring representativeness. In the long run, data collection needs to be based on standardised reporting because, as the market grows, surveys will become increasingly expensive.

5.7. Possible future approaches for data collection

Different players are engaged in collecting data on SII components from different angles, with different approaches and using different definitions. The plethora of new initiatives and reports attempting to size the SII market is a positive trend and suggests growing interest in understanding SII. However it makes it harder to identify key sources of data and compare and consolidate estimates. In addition, effort duplication and data overlapping is a serious risk. Collaboration between those players currently involved in data collection efforts is key. Some steps in this direction are already being taken. For example, the "Social Investment Research Council" was recently created in the United Kingdom to consolidate research efforts and avoid duplication.[9] Also, efforts to increase data comparability across countries are being made through initiatives such as the GIIN or the work of the SIITF.

To ensure comparability across data collection efforts taking place in different geographies, metadata is crucial as it helps understanding what exactly is available and how detailed are currently available data. This is particularly relevant when SII definitions are not yet established. Moreover, transparency requirements can help moving towards common standards. Such transparency requirements might be burdensome on the different players involved in the market, but they necessarily come with a standardisation exercise, whose benefits can outweigh the costs. It is however important to note that standards might limit the scope for innovation. The right balance should be found so that the standardisation procedure does not gridlock the SII market and prevents it from further innovating and growing.

A system based on automatic reporting would bring some advantages in terms of coverage and quality of the data. Such data can then be complemented with further information collected via surveys for specific purposes. Data reporting can be very costly for companies (especially for small social businesses), investors, intermediaries, while a significant part of the data obtained might end up not being used. It is important to note that the direct benefits SII players accrue from reporting are relatively small, so the adequate incentive mechanism needs to be put in place.

Requiring certification is an approach that can work as an incentive for companies to make the effort to report. By being certified (see Box 5.6 for the case of B-corp certification procedure), social enterprises gain more visibility as was as it sends a positive signal to potential investors. The certification procedure by B-corp is burdensome as it involves a survey, an interview, request for documentation and random checks, but it guarantees high data quality standards.

Certification can also have positive effects in terms of more formalised outcome measurement practices that support the development of the SII market. However, from the viewpoint of businesses, certification can significantly increase reporting costs, thus the benefits of a move towards more stringent certification procedures should also be balanced against the increased regulatory burden. The certification requirements necessarily need to be mandated by public authorities in each country and possibly coordinated internationally. Public authorities can also play a role though regulation because it necessarily implies a standardisation exercise. Since SII is a new concept, data collection agencies, regulators and authorities have not yet developed standardised and internationally comparable definitions and classifications that would allow a systematic collection of data.

Box 5.6. **Certification and labels: B-corp example**

B-Corporation is a NPI that certifies for-profit companies according to their practices in terms of achieving social impact. The certification is based on a set of company information obtained through an online survey (done in collaboration with CASE i3, Box 5.5). Scores are attributed to companies according to a previously set methodology that values survey answers (thus company characteristics) differently through a weighting procedure.

Table 5.7. **Snapshot of the B-corp profile information**

Name	City	State/ Province	Industry	Overall score	Accountability	Beneficial method	Local community
***	San Francisco	CA	NULL	137.4	16.8	NULL	NULL
***	Poulsboro	WA	Consumer products and services: housewares	NULL	NULL	NULL	NULL
***	Richmond	BC	NULL	NULL	NULL	29.7	2.1
***	Vancouver	BC	Technology: information technology services	NULL	NULL	NULL	NULL
***	Belvedere	CA	NULL	NULL	NULL	50.7	5.2
***	Philadelphia	PA	NULL	83.5	8	27.2	6.1
***	Fremont	CA	NULL	145.2	23.6	NULL	NULL
***	Haleiwa	HI	NULL	88.1	7.5	NULL	NULL

Notes: Only four variables out of 133 are shown here. The variable *Overall Score* is an aggregation of the 133 scores. The names of the companies are omitted here for anonymity purposes. The maximum score is 200 and only companies over the 80 points threshold can be considered a B-corp.

Source: B-Corp Profile information available at: http://sites.duke.edu/casei3/files/2013/03/B-Corp-Profile-Information.xlsx (accessed on 25 July 2014).

Box 5.6. **Certification and labels: B-corp example (cont.)**

For example a question on the commitment to achieve social impact embedded in the company's mission is given a higher weight than a different question regarding stakeholder engagement. Other characteristics include different indicators on transparency, reporting, treatment of employees, work environment, the type of impact, targeted populations, community involvement and impact, *inter alia*. In total, around 130 company characteristics are surveyed through an equal number of questions.

Base on the set of predetermined scores, companies are profiled and evaluated across the different set of characteristics, after which they are given a final overall score that will be the basis for the eligibility to become a B-corp (above a certain global score threshold. To become a B-corp, companies are also required to make amendments to the articles of incorporation, explicitly recognising the importance of other stakeholders beyond shareholders. A snapshot of the profile information is provided in the table below. After a there is a clarification procedure through which B-corp reviews the data provided together with the company. This and further quality checks (e.g. requests for official documents) are time and resource consuming, but help ensuring that the data is accurate.

Source: B-Corporation website, available at: www.bcorporation.net/.

Certification may also evolve to a rating system. GIIRS is a recent initiative that aims at working as a rating organisation specialised in SII (see Section 5.4.3 for details on GIIRS data collection).[10] Such an approach is very important because it allows increasing informational efficiency, insofar as the creation of an additional layer of information asymmetry is avoided.

Benchmarking is regarded to be one important but challenging aspect for investors in SII (Saltuk et al., 2011). Currently, it is very difficult to assess the risk-return profile of a social impact investment. For investments in mainstream capital markets, several indexes exist, against which asset performance can be benchmarked. However, in SII performance measures go beyond the common valuation of expected returns and foreseeable risks. Social outcomes create a wedge between the private pecuniary outcome and the benefits that accrue the larger society.

It is important to allow investors to factor social impact into investment decisions, while rating systems should help clarifying and tracking impact risk (WGAA, 2014). Both social impact and impact risk should feature in a benchmark for SII. A number of initiatives such as GIIRS or Engaged X have been working towards creating benchmarks for the SII market that incorporate metrics for social impacts and access risks.

Further work to develop robust and comparable impact measurement practices (in delivery organisations and for investors) can also help building the evidence base. The Impact Measurement working group set a number of principles required to work towards an "impact measurement convention" in the future. This would ensure a standardised approach for impact measurement and envisage a reporting system that ensures the availability of quality impact data (WGIM). The governance model of such process is however not yet clear. This would in principle entail a commitment from governments and industry to set up a working group with representatives from governments and industry and a steering committee that would agree upon the common impact measurement language, guidelines, and data infrastructure. International organisations could provide the appropriate forum for such discussion.

As the SII market continues to grow in the future, commercial data providers that provide information for investors might be increasingly interested in compiling SII information if selling SII data becomes a viable business. Some of these commercial data providers have already seen value in gathering information on certain SII-related components. For example, Factset compiles information on the NPI sector, despite there is a very strong geographical bias towards the United States.[11] Given the embryonic state of the SII market, the policy relevance of SII models and the role that Governments might play in these initial stages, it would be important that efforts are made to collect (and share) systematic data within an open-data approach.

Alternative strategies to gathering SII data were also discussed at the OECD SII expert meetings. These included polls, community feedback mechanisms and tapping into big data. Even though these approaches can provide rich and extensive information, data quality control and verification is extremely challenging.

Collecting data is costly and its value is often not fully appreciated by the industry and/or policymakers. While costs should be minimised and data collection efficiency strived for, it is clear that further resources should be deployed into gathering the evidence base. For example, small grants or lottery-type prizes can be provided as an additional incentive for organisations to report data (Bloom and Clark, 2011). The efforts need to be made jointly between all SII market actors. Better data would be important for delivery organisations that would get more visibility, investors that would know better where to allocate their money, intermediaries that would be able to provide a better offer of investment products, as well as policymakers to fully understand whether the SII model is superior and should be further supported and incentivised.

Providing comprehensive information can be a significant burden for delivery organisations. However, requiring specific information (e.g. impact measurement) for funding purposes is a key incentive for investee reporting that can be aligned with investor interests. Further efforts are needed to embed a data reporting culture in delivery organisations – and also in supply side organisations and intermediaries. Incentives for investor reporting, likely via intermediaries or investors networks, can include disclosure of part of the available data or even granting access to a dataset on potential SII investment. Also, ensuring that investors report actual (instead of potential) returns is essential to guaranteed data reliability. Incentives based on data exchange arrangements can also be important to bring SII intermediaries together in a platform or a network for data exchange.

Data collection also requires technological infrastructure. It is important to have a simple infrastructure where all data can be put in. A possible way to further advance on data collection and comparability in the long run could be to work towards creating a platform in which players currently engaged in data collection (from the different parts of the SII framework) could come together and share information.

At a first stage, increased collaboration among a few key players through meetings to share experience and data can contribute to further advancing the understanding about the SII market. At the OECD SII Expert Meetings it was noted that the group of experts could be drawn upon to help move beyond proprietary data, generate consensus and have a "clear" model for data collection. It would be important that data shared in such platform is made freely available on an open-source basis, keeping in mind that organisations collecting data also have to appropriate some value from their efforts.

Optimal data on SII is currently not feasible to obtain, but it is important to push the discussion forward. It is however important to bear in mind that data collection should not become an end in itself and the purposes for data collection need to be *a priori* clear. The bulk of systematic evidence on SII will likely come from private data sources in earlier stages of market development. Fostering the collaboration between the different organisations collecting SII data through in surveys, polls and other approaches is key. While reaching a common understanding about definitions is vital, agreeing on a methodology to collect comparable cross-country data could provide the evidence base for a better understanding of the SII market. It can also help in the analysis of the role that policymaking can play in this area. Drawing upon private and other types of finance to meet public objectives is an opportunity, but one which requires a good understanding of the incentives of the different players involved.

Notes

1. The OECD sought to gather information on SII data sources and data collection processes. The research process included reviewing the academic literature that focuses on SII-related data, industry reports that bring together information on the size and scope of SII in the different countries and information from other data sources. The OECD conducted further research to provide an overview of existing SII data sources and data collection approaches, pinpointing main data-related challenges.

2. Returns and other relevant data associated with SII flows is considered here to be part of transactions.

3. Oltreventure's directory can be found at www.oltreventure.com/index.php/investimenti/riepilogo. ClearlySo provides a directory of social enterprises around the world, available at www.clearlyso.com/directory.html.

4. Information on the United Kingdom's Social investment tax relief is available at https://www.gov.uk/government/publications/social-investment-tax-relief-factsheet/social-investment-tax-relief.

5. Available at: http://apps.irs.gov/app/eos/forwardToPub78Download.do.

6. Sample size varied by region (between 16 and 145 SEOs). Response rates where unknown in many regions due to lack of information on the number of surveys distributed. Where available, response rates varied between 6.4% and 17.7%.

7. Information on the Expert Group on Social Entrepreneurship can be found at: http://ec.europa.eu/internal_market/social_business/expert-group/index_en.htm.

8. Information on the EMES network can be found at www.emes.net/. Information from the European project TEPSIE is available at www.tepsie.eu/.

9. The Social Investment Research Council is a joint venture between Big Society Capital, Big Lottery Fund, City of London, Citi and the Cabinet Office.

10. Information available at http://giirs.org/.

11. A dataset obtained from Factset comprises 14 363 NPIs of which 97% are based in the United States. Over 89% are owned by another NPI, around 9% by foundations and the remaining 2% by other types of companies

(notoriously business ventures in the private sphere). Even for the United States, this dataset only represents about 2% of the total number of *Organizations Eligible to Receive Tax - Deductible Charitable Contributions* (IRS, available at: http://apps.irs.gov/app/eos/forwardToPub78Download.do).

References

Addis, R., J. McLeod, and A. Raine (2013), "IMPACT Australia: Investment for Social and Economic Benefit", Australian Government, Department of Education, Employment and Workplace Relations, November.

Alcock, P., R., Millar, K., Hall, F., Lyon, A., Nicholls, and M., Gabriel (2012), "Start-up and Growth: National Evaluation of the Social Enterprise Investment Fund (SEIF)", London: Department of Health Policy Research Programme (PRP). forthcoming.

Anttonen, A., and L. Häikiö (2011), "Care 'going market': Finnish elderly-care policies in transition", *Nordic Journal of Social Research*, 2.

Blazy, C. (2011), "Le financement des entreprises sociales-une comparaison France-Californie: Accès aux fonds propres et aux financements moyen terme", MPRA paper No. 33220, Munich, Germany.

Bloom, P. and C. Clark (2011), "The Challenges of Creating Databases To Support Rigorous Research in Social Entrepreneurship" Center for the Advancement of Social Entrepreneurship, Fuqua School of Business Duke University Durham, NC, November.

Borzaga, C., Depedri, S. and E. Tortia (2010), "Testing the distributive effects of social enterprises: the case of Italy", *Social capital, Corporate social responsibility, Economic Behaviour and Performance, Basingstoke: Palgrave MacMillan,*

Brown, A. and Swersky, A. (2012), "The First Billion: A forecast of social investment demand", Boston Consulting Group, London, September.

Brown, A. and W. Norman (2011), "Lighting the touchpaper: Growing the Market for Social Investment in England", Boston Consulting Group and Young Foundation, London, November.

City of London (2013), "The role of tax incentives in encouraging social investment", Report prepared for the City of London and Big society Capital by Worthstone assisted by Wragge & Co LLP, March.

Chua, C., A. Gupta, V. Hsu, J. Jimenez and Y. Li (2011), "Beyond the Margin: Redirecting Asia's Capitalism", Advantage Ventures, August.

Clark, C., J. Emerson and B. Thornley (2013), "Impact Investing 2.0: The Way Forward – Insight from 12 Outstanding Funds", Pacific Community Ventures, Inc., ImpactAssets, and Duke University's Fuqua School of Business, November.

DTI (2002), "Social enterprise: a strategy for success", London: Department for Trade and Industry.

ECOTEC (2003), "Guidance on mapping social enterprise", London: Department for Trade and Industry.

Elson, P. and P. Hall (2013), "Ploughing the fields: Provincial surveys of social enterprises in Canada", 4th EMES International Research Conference on Social Enterprise, Liège, Belgium, July.

Fedele, A and R. Miniaci (2010). Do social enterprises finance their investments differently from for-profit firms? The case of social residential services in Italy. *Journal of Social Entrepreneurship*, 1(2), 174-189.

Florek, N. (2013), "Enabling social enterprise through regulatory innovation: a case study from the United Kingdom." *Journal of Sustainable Finance & Investment* 3(2): 155-175.

Freireich, J. and K. Fulton (2009), "Investing for Social and Environmental Impact: A Design for Catalyzing an Emerging Industry", Monitor Institute, January.

GHK (2013), "Growing the Social Investment Market: The Landscape and Economic Impact" report prepared for the City of London, Big Lottery Fund, Big Society Capital, and Her Majesty's Government by ICF GHK in association with BMG Research, July.

GIIN (2014), Global Impact Investing Network website. Available at: www.thegiin.org/cgi-bin/iowa/resources/about/index.html (accessed 15 May 2014).

Glänzel, G., Krlev, G., Schmitz, B. and G. Mildenberger (2013), "Report on the feasibility and opportunities of using various instruments for capitalising social innovators" TEPSIE, European Commission – 7th Framework Programme, Brussels: European Commission, DG Research

Harji, K. J. Reynolds, H. Best and M. Jeyaloganathan (2014), "State of the Nation: Impact Investing in Canada", MaRS Centre for Impact Investing and Purpose Capital, March. Available at: www.marsdd.com/mars-library/impact-investing-in-canada-state-of-the-nation/.

Hazenberg, R., F., Seddon, A. and S. Denny (2013), “Intermediary perceptions of investment readiness in the social investment market”, Seventeenth Annual Conference of the International Research Society for Public Management, Prague,CzechRepublic,10-12April

HM Government, United Kingdom (2013), “G8 Social Impact Investment Forum: Outputs and Agreed Actions”, UK Cabinet Office, London, July.

Hope Consulting (2010), “Money for good: the US market for impact investments and charitable gifts from individual donors and investors”, July.

IFF Research (2005), “A survey of social enterprises across the UK”, London: Small Business Service.

Kerlin, J. (2010), "A comparative analysis of the global emergence of social enterprise", *VOLUNTAS: International Journal of Voluntary and Nonprofit Organizations* 21, no. 2 (2010): 162-179.

La Croix (2014), “Baromètre de la finance solidaire”, Finansol and La Croix, May.

Lyon, F. and L. Sepulveda (2009), “Mapping social enterprises: past approaches, challenges and future directions”, *Social Enterprise Journal*, 5(1), 83-94.

Lyon, F., M., Gabriel, and R. Millar (2010), “Social Enterprise Investment Fund Evaluation-Phase one: scoping, review and methodology development”, Working Paper. TSRC and Health Services Management Centre at the University of Birmingham, Birmingham.

Mendell, M. and E. Barbosa (2013), “Impact investing: a preliminary analysis of emergent primary and secondary exchange platforms”, *Journal of Sustainable Finance & Investment*, 3(2):111-23

Nicholls, A. (2010a), “The institutionalization of social investment: The interplay of investment logics and investor rationalities”, *Journal of social entrepreneurship*, *1*(1), 70-100.

Nicholls (2010b), “The landscape of social investment in the UK”, Working Paper. TSRC and Health Services Management Centre at the University of Birmingham, Birmingham.

Noya, A.(ed.) (2009),*The Changing Boundaries of Social Enterprises*, Local Economic and Employment Development (LEED), OECD Publishing, http://dx.doi.org/10.1787/9789264055513-en.

OECD (2013f), "Institutional investors indicators", OECD Institutional Investors Statistics (database), http://dx.doi.org/10.1787/data-00679-en (accessed 7 August 2014).

OECD (2013g) "Job Creation through the Social Economy and Social Entrepreneurship", OECD LEED Programme (Local Economic and Employment Development).

Saltuk, Y., A. Idrissi, A. Bouri, A. Mudaliar, and H. Schiff (2014), "Spotlight on the Market: The Impact Investor Survey", Global Social Finance, J.P. Morgan and the Global Impact Investing Network, London, 2 May.

Saltuk, Y, A. Bouri, A. Mudaliar and M. Pease (2013), "Perspectives on Progress: The Impact Investor Survey", Global Social Finance, J.P. Morgan and the Global Impact Investing Network, London, January 7.

Saltuk, Y., A. Bouri, and G. Leung (2011), "Insight into the Impact Investment Market: An in-depth analysis of investor perspectives and over 2,200 transactions", JP Morgan and the Global Impact Investing Network, New York, December.

Smith, S. and J., Rothbaum (2013), "Cooperatives in a Global Economy: Key Economic Issues, Recent Trends, and Potential for Development", IZA Policy Paper No. 68.

Teasdale, S., Lyon, F. and R. Baldock (2013), "Playing with numbers: a methodological critique of the social enterprise growth myth", *Journal of Social Entrepreneurship*, 4(2), 113-131.

UN (2003), "Handbook on Non-profit institutions in the system of National Accounts". United Nations. Statistical Division, United Nations Publications.

Unicredit Foundation (2012) "Ricerca sul valore economic del Terzo Settore in Italia", Unicredit Foundation, April 2012. Available at: www.forumterzosettore.it/multimedia/allegati/Ricerca.pdf.

Weber, M. and B. Scheck (2012), "Impact Investing in Deutschland: Bestandsaufnahme und Handlungsanweisungen zur Weiterentwicklung", Impact in Motion and Bertelsmann Foundation, December. Available at www.impactinmotion.com/wp/wp-content/uploads/2013/05/Impact-Investing-in-Detschland_08052013.pdf.

Wells, P. (2012) "Understanding social investment policy: evidence from the evaluation of Futurebuilders in England", *Voluntary Sector Review*, *3*(2), 157-177.

Wilkinson, C. (2014), "A map of social enterprises and their eco-systems in Europe", ICF International, Forthcoming.

Wilson, K. E. (2014), "New Investment Approaches for Addressing Social and Economic Challenges", OECD Science, Technology and Industry Policy Papers, No. 15, OECD Publishing, http://dx.doi.org/10.1787/5jz2bz8g00jj-en.

Annex 5.1. List of existing data sources

This list of data sources only includes organisations that currently provide raw data on SII. Therefore, only organisations that actually provide either raw data or data in reports were included on the list. Organisations that may have important links to SII market players and could potentially serve as partners in future data collection efforts are not necessarily included on the list, insofar as they do not currently provide data.

In addition, some of the data sources described as currently providing raw data do not necessarily publicly disclose the information. Nevertheless, they feature on the list because information could, in principle, be shared under certain conditions. Some organisations have been collecting data, but have not yet disclosed any data-related information (e.g. Maximpact). In such cases a decision to include them on the list was based on the fact they have data and will potentially be disclosing it in the near future.

Governmental sources, information from NSOs and sources available from financial system supervisory and regulatory bodies were not included here to avoid multiple entries (one per country for each type of organisation). The list focuses on data that are, in general, more challenging to obtain and that require further discussion and contribution from SII data experts. Nevertheless, the potential of data collection from some of the sources omitted in the list is also discussed in this note.

Provider	Type of data (ecosystem)	Geography	Link
SESS	Demand	CAN - local	www.sess.ca/english/report/
TEPSIE	Demand	Europe	www.tepsie.eu/
Cooperative Association Germany	Demand	GER	www.dgrv.de/en/home.html
ClearlySo	Demand	Global	https://www.clearlyso.com
Social Progress Imperative	Demand	Global	www.socialprogressimperative.org/
IRIS	Demand	Global - focus US; UK	http://iris.thegiin.org/

Provider	Type of data (ecosystem)	Geography	Link
B-Corporation	Demand	Global - focus USA	www.bcorporation.net/what-are-b-corps/why-b-corps-matter
Unicredit	Demand	ITA	www.forumterzosettore.it/multimedia/allegati/Ricerca.pdf
IRIS (Italian)	Demand	ITA	http://irisnetwork.it/
CIC regulator	Demand	UK	www.bis.gov.uk/CICREGULATOR
Social Enterprise UK	Demand	UK	www.socialenterprise.org.uk/policy-campaigns/policy/research
CASE at Duke University	Demand	USA	http://sites.duke.edu/casei3/for-researchers-2/case-i3-b-lab-and-giirs-research-project/
Nonprofit Finance Fund	Demand	USA	http://nonprofitfinancefund.org/tools-resources
Comparative non-profit sector project	Demand	Global	http://ccss.jhu.edu/research-projects/comparative-nonprofit-sector
Social Enterprise Alliance (SEA)	Demand	USA	https://www.se-alliance.org/
Australian Charities and Not-for-Profits Commission (ACNC)	Demand	AUS	www.acnc.gov.au/
GIIRS	Demand and supply	Global	http://giirs.org/for-investors/company-directory http://giirs.org/for-investors/fund-directory
Caisse des Dépôts	Intermediaries/ transactions	FRA	www.caissedesdepots.fr/activite/domaines-daction/investissements-davenir/financement-de-leconomie-sociale-et-solidaire.html
Finansol	Intermediaries/ transactions	FRA	www.finansol.org/_dwl/zoom-finance-solidaire.pdf
Bpifrance	Intermediaries/ transactions	FRA	www.bpifrance.fr/
NExT SSE	Intermediaries/ transactions	GER	www.nextsse.com/home/news-events/
Impact Assets	Intermediaries/ transactions	Global	www.impactassets.org/
Monitor institute	Intermediaries/ transactions	Global	monitorinstitute.com/what-we-think/#
Omydiar Network	Intermediaries/ transactions	Global	www.omidyar.com/
GIIN/Impact Base	Intermediaries/ transactions	Global	www.impactbase.org/
JP Morgan/GIIN	Intermediaries/ transactions	Global	www.thegiin.org/
Maximpact	Intermediaries/ transactions	Global	www.maximpact.com/
Engaged investment	Intermediaries/ transactions	Global	www.engagedinvestment.com/

Provider	Type of data (ecosystem)	Geography	Link
Toniic	Intermediaries/ transactions	Global	www.toniic.com/
TRIODOS Bank	Intermediaries/ transactions	Global- focus Europe	www.triodos.com/en/about-triodos-bank/
Oltre Venture	Intermediaries/ transactions	ITA	www.oltreventure.com/oltre-1-investimenti/
BSC- Big Society Capital	Intermediaries/ transactions	UK	www.bigsocietycapital.com/
Community Development Finance Association (CDFA)	Intermediaries/ transactions	UK	www.cdfa.org.uk/
CDFI FUND	Intermediaries/ transactions	USA	www.cdfifund.gov/
Massolution	Intermediaries/ transactions	USA	www.massolution.com/
National Community Investment Fund (NCIF)	Intermediaries/ transactions	USA	www.ncif.org/
Instiglio	Intermediaries/ transactions		www.instiglio.org/en/sibs-worldwide/
EVPA	Intermediaries/ transactions	Europe	http://evpa.eu.com/knowledge-centre/
AVPN	Intermediaries/ transactions	Asia	https://avpn.asia/
Impact in Motion	Supply and intermediaries/ transactions	GER	http://impactinmotion.com/
Philantropy Australia	Supply	AUS	www.philanthropy.org.au/tools-resources/publications/
Productivity Commission	Supply	AUS	www.pc.gov.au/publications/publications?queries_by_type_query=Publication
European Foundation Centre	Supply	Europe	www.efc.be/
Fondation de France	Supply	FRA	www.fondationdefrance.org/Outils/Mediatheque/Etudes-de-l-Observatoire
Centre Français de Fonds et Fondations	Supply	FRA	www.centre-francais-fondations.org/ressources-pratiques/gerer-ou-faire-vivre-un-fonds-ou-une-fondation/gestion-patrimoniale/gestion-financiere/vers-de-nouveaux-modes-de-selection-des-placements/impact-investing
Association of German Foundations	Supply	GER	www.stiftungen.org/en/association-of-german-foundations.html
ACRI	Supply	ITA	https://www.acri.it/

Provider	Type of data (ecosystem)	Geography	Link
The Japan Foundation Center	Supply	JAP	www.jfc.or.jp/eibun/e_index.html
GOV_UK	Supply	UK	http://data.gov.uk/dataset/social-investment-and-foundations
Association of charitable foundations	Supply	UK	www.acf.org.uk/
Foundation Center	Supply	USA	http://fconline.foundationcenter.org/
Impact Investing Australia	Overall	AUS	http://impactinvestingaustralia.com/resources/
Purpose Capital	Overall	CAN	http://purposecap.com/
MaRS Centre for Impact Investing	Overall	Global	http://impactinvesting.marsdd.com/
IIPC	Overall	Global	http://iipcollaborative.org/about/iipc-research/
Pacific Community Ventures	Overall	Global	www.pacificcommunityventures.org/category/publications/
Stanford Social Innovation Review	Overall	Global	www.ssireview.org/topics/category/impact_investing
Social Impact Analysts Association	Overall	Global - focus EU; CAN	www.siaassociation.org/
BCG	Overall	Global-focus UK	www.bcg.com/expertise_impact/PublicationDetails.aspx?id=tcm:12-115600&mid
The City of London	Overall	UK	www.cityoflondon.gov.uk/business/supporting-local-communities/Pages/supporting-social-enterprise.aspx
OECD	Demand, supply and enabling environment	Global-focus OECD	http://stats.oecd.org/
IMF	Supply	Global	www.imf.org/external/data.htm
World Bank	Demand, supply and enabling environment	Global	http://data.worldbank.org/
World Values Survey	Enabling environment	Global	www.worldvaluessurvey.org/wvs.jsp
European Social Survey	Enabling environment	Europe	www.europeansocialsurvey.org/
Eurofund	Enabling environment	Europe	www.eurofound.europa.eu/publications/htmlfiles/ef1361.htm
Social Progress Imperative	Enabling environment	Global	www.socialprogressimperative.org/data/spi

Source: OECD, based on desk research.

Annex 5.2. List of OECD data sources relevant to SII

Database	Type	Examples	Link
Social expenditure	Spending	Public/private expenditure Cash/kind expenditures Breakdown by social area	www.oecd.org/els/social/expenditure
Institutional investor statistics	Supply	Financial assets	http://stats.oecd.org/Index.aspx?DataSetCode=7IA#
How's Life Indicators	Needs	Quality of support network; homicide rate	http://stats.oecd.org/OECDStat_Metadata/ShowMetadata.ashx?Dataset=BLI&ShowOnWeb=true&Lang=en
Tax/Benefits	Spending	Social contributions; housing benefits	http://stats.oecd.org/BrandedView.aspx?oecd_bv_id=tax-data-en&doi=data-00201-en
Social indicators	Needs	Old age support rate; prison population	www.oecd.org/els/soc/societyataglance.htm
National accounts	Spending	NPIs serving households	www.oecd.org/std/na/
Health indicators	Spending and needs	Financing health expenditure Life expectancy; infant health	http://stats.oecd.org/index.aspx?DataSetCode=HEALTH_STAT
Education indicators	Spending and needs	Expenditure by funding source Literacy scores Education expenditure	http://stats.oecd.org/BrandedView.aspx?oecd_bv_id=edu-data-en&doi=edu-db-data-en ; and http://gpseducation.oecd.org/IndicatorExplorer
Product market Regulation	Regulation	Scope of government in specific sectors Specific barriers to entrepreneurship	www.oecd.org/economy/growth/indicatorsofproductmarketregulationhomepage.htm
Entrepreneurship indicators	Demand	Entrepreneurial culture	www.oecd-ilibrary.org/industry-and-services/entrepreneurship-at-a-glance-2013_entrepreneur_aag-2013-en
Structural indicators	Supply Demand	Financial sector (C65T74) Community, social and personal services (C75T99)	www.oecd.org/sti/ind/stanstructuralanalysisdatabase.htm
Financing scoreboard	Supply	Trends in SME loans Government guarantees	www.oecd-ilibrary.org/industry-and-services/financing-smes-and-entrepreneurs_23065265
Development co-operation	Supply	Flows: project-type interventions	http://dotstat.oecd.org/inventory.aspx?datasetcode=TABLE1
Development aid	Supply	Aid	www.oecd.org/dac/stats/
Network of foundations	Supply	Foundations	www.oecd.org/site/netfwd/

Source: OECD.

Table A.5.1. Types of Non-Profit Institutions

1. Culture and recreation	1 100 Culture and arts 1 200 Sports 1 300 Other recreation and social clubs
2. Education and research	2 100 Primary and secondary education 2 200 Higher education 2 300 Other education 2 400 Research
3. Health	3 100 Hospitals and rehabilitation 3 200 Nursing homes 3 300 Mental health and crisis intervention 3 400 Other health services
4. Social services	4 100 Social services 4 200 Emergency and relief 4 300 Income support and maintenance
5. Environment	5 100 Environment 5 200 Animal protection
6 Development and housing	6 100 Economic, social and community development 6 200 Housing 6 300 Employment and training
7. Law, advocacy and politics	7 100 Civic and advocacy organisations 7 200 Law and legal services 7 300 Political organisations
8. Philanthropic intermediaries and voluntarism promotion	8 100 Grant-making Foundations 8 200 Other philanthropic intermediaries and voluntarism promotion
9. International	9 100 International activities
10. Religion	10 100 Religious congregations and associations
11. Business and professional associations, unions	11 100 Business associations 11 200 Professional associations 11 300 Labour unions
12. Not elsewhere classified	12 100 Not elsewhere classified

Source: UN (2003).

Chapter 6

Policy actions and implications

This chapter provides an overview of different types of policy actions to support the Social Impact Investment market taken to date. It reviews the challenges for policymakers planning to take actions to support this nascent field and makes recommendations focusing on the steps required to build the evidence base. These including developing common definitions, building the necessary data infrastructure and primary impact measurement as well as evaluation of broader social outcomes.

6.1. Policy actions and implications

There are a number of market failures in social impact investment. The most fundamental failure relates to the very nature of social impact investment. The social returns generated from social impact investments are primarily external to both the investor and the investee, with the primary beneficiaries being those groups whose needs are being targeted, or accrue to society as a whole. Given market inefficiencies, these externalities are not priced into social impact investment transactions (HM Government, 2011).

However, in addition to this there are failures which relate to the functioning of the market itself. As in the mainstream financial markets, there are information asymmetries between investors and investees. These asymmetries are further compounded by the lack of commonly accepted standards for measuring social impact investment, confusion of terminology and lack of information about both existing investment provision as well as related government policy (HM Government, 2011). There is also imperfect competition in the market due to high transaction costs as well as the lack of intermediaries in the form of brokers, advisors, exchanges and other market mechanisms.

The public sector can play a catalytic role in the social impact investment market in terms of creating a conducive regulatory environment, encouraging greater transparency and taking concrete steps to help develop the market. Actions can be taken at the international, national or local level. However, actions initiated in one country or region may not be appropriate for another – policy objectives, experience and local context must be taken into account.

New and/or inefficient markets may benefit from government involvement. Certainly, the social impact investment market is in its early days and needs to find scalable models. As policy makers seek to facilitate the development of the market, they should keep in mind that public support should be a catalyst and avoid "crowding out" of the private sector in order to ensure the creation of a sustainable market. Government intervention, while well-meaning, can have unintended consequences.

6.2. Policy actions to date

There are various actions that governments could take to support SII, ranging from indirect to direct. Indirect actions can include ensuring that the necessary legal frameworks and structures are in place including the streamlining of regulations and requirements for investment (Thornley et al, 2011). Direct actions can include various forms of support to social ventures and facilitating the development of intermediaries. It should also be noted that, the absence of any action can also have implications for the market.

The Impact Investing Policy Collaborative (IIPC) has developed a framework which aims to create a guide for policy makers seeking to build the social impact investment market in their countries or communities. This includes looking at the government's role as a market builder, participant and steward. The framework builds upon earlier work by the World Economic Forum (WEF, 2012) as well as upon *The London Principles,*[1] a set of guidelines intended to assist governments considering impact investing as a tool to address social objectives, developed by the IIPC in collaboration with policymakers, researchers and other stakeholders in July 2013.

The recent Social Impact Investment Taskforce and National Advisory Board reports highlighted actions that have been taken to date in the G7 countries and Australia.[2] Annex 6.1 summarises some of these policy actions. Table 6.1 below attempts to provide a summary of the longer list of policy actions outlined in Annex 6.1 within the framework of the social impact investment ecosystem discussed in Chapter 2 (demand, supply, intermediaries and regulatory/enabling environment).

Table 6.1. **Examples of types of policy actions taken in G7 countries and Australia**

Supply	Demand	Tax and regulation	Intermediaries	Other
Social Enterprise Development and Investment Funds (Australia) Small Business Investment Company Impact Investment Fund (United States)	Social Innovation Forum (Japan) Investment and Contract Readiness Fund (United Kingdom)	Loi n° 2014-856 : Économie sociale et solidaire (France) Legge delega di riforma del Terzo Settore (Italy)	SVX trading platform (Ontario, Canada) Big Society Capital (United Kingdom)	Unit Cost Database (United Kingdom) Community Reinvestment Act (United States)

Source: OECD, based on National Advisory Board (NAB) reports – NAB_AUS (2014), NAB_CAN (2014), NAB_GER (2014), NAB_FRA (2014), NAB_ITA (2014), NAB_JAP (2014), NAB_UK (2014), NAB_US (2014).

Policy actions in some of these countries have addressed regulatory issues, notably in terms of setting up legal structures to accommodate SII-specific types of market actors. Also, several policy interventions have sought to enhance SII supply. Some governments have provided support through tax credits (and tax-advantaged funds), guarantees or subsidies, established and co-invested in SII funds. Other governments have focused on developing the social impact investment market infrastructure through the creation of intermediaries such as SII wholesale banks, exchanges (or trading platforms) and other channels to facilitate the links between supply and demand for SII (investors and delivery organisations). Additionally some have sought to stimulate SII demand by providing support to delivery organisations/ investees through technical assistance or by encouraging procurement.

While there have been an increasing set of policy actions in the social impact investment market, to date, there have only been a few evaluations, including the ICRF evaluation referenced in Chapter 2 and the SIB evaluation described later in this chapter. This is also due to the fact that many of these policy actions are relatively new. The Social Impact Investment Taskforce and the NABs have helped to highlight the set of existing policy actions which has facilitated discussions about how these and other policies are working.

There are also several policy instruments that, while affecting SII, do not necessarily target the SII ecosystem (e.g. seed funds; regulations on institutional investors' asset allocation and risk). When devising broader policy instruments, it is important that governments take into consideration potential favouring or hindering effects upon the SII market and balance them against expected outcomes in other areas of the economy.

Patience and long-term support is needed to develop a market. Creating and investing in new innovative social ventures and building supporting ecosystem takes time and results might only be seen after 10 years or more (HM Government, 2013c). Policy is long-term but politics can be short-term so there is a danger that the increased level of government interest and involvement in this topic might decline in the shorter term if the necessary results are not forthcoming.

Given the plethora of recent reports outlining a broad set of policy recommendations (SIITF, Working Groups, NABs, IIPC, etc.), the recommendations below address how to build the evidence base, which is the overall focus of this report.

6.3. Recommended policy actions for building the evidence base

As social challenges mount and existing approaches are unable to keep up amidst continued pressure on government budgets, social impact investment provides an opportunity to develop new approaches to address social and economic challenges. However, given that SII is a nascent field, concrete evidence is needed in terms of its impact to date. In particular, further work is needed to demonstrate the gains from the SII approach, compared to existing social service delivery models. Therefore our recommendations focus on building the evidence base, including developing a common agreement on definitions, committing to building the necessary infrastructure for coordinated data collection processes, furthering efforts on the measurement of social outcomes and evaluation of policy.

Given that additional, and more effective, funding is needed to address the increasing social challenges facing society, governments in a number of countries are demonstrating interest in exploring the opportunities that SII could also provide in terms of improved social service delivery. In fact, as described in Section 6.2, some countries have already set up policies to facilitate the development of SII markets. As there is limited evidence to date in terms of what works and what doesn't, this section outlines some recommendations in terms of building the evidence base and suggestions regarding key points for policy makers to keep in mind, particularly in terms of outcome measures and evaluation of policies. Further analysis is needed in terms of specific approaches to SII, looking at a variety of instruments and sector-specific developments. This would help develop a better understanding of which approaches seem to be working and help build and share experiences which could later lead to the scaling up of successful cases.

6.3.1. Developing common definitions

A stronger evidence base, both in terms of the level of market activity as well as the impact of SII, is critical to increasing engagement in the market and encouraging a global market to develop (HM Government, 2013c). This includes a better and more accurate understanding of the size, scope and potential of the market. To develop a clearer view on the market, common definitions, language and frameworks are necessary.

As outlined in Chapter 3, there is broad agreement in the market regarding the core characteristics of SII, however, less agreement on the next level of detail, the key attributes of each of the characteristics. More importantly, there has been little discussion to date of where to "draw the line" on SII in terms of thresholds or eligibility of the various attributes. Chapter 3 of this paper makes some recommendations but further discussion is needed, on an international level, to develop a common agreement. To that end, international organisations, such as the OECD, can provide a continued forum for debate.

6.3.2. Building the necessary data infrastructure

Policy makers can help in raising awareness and understanding about social impact investment by supporting systematic research and data collection. However, while a growing number of industry reports have been supported, not enough attention has been paid to date on supporting the necessary data infrastructure needed to develop standardised data reporting and collection processes. These are critical for building the evidence base for SII and the groundwork needs to be laid for this as early as possible.

More and coordinated data collection is needed to more effectively monitor developments in the market. Data collection processes which allow for wider comparability, including across countries, would also be useful

(Addis et al, 2013). There are data collection efforts within individual organisations and some broader pilot efforts but to date there has not been a forum for discussing how to standardise data collection globally. The OECD expert meetings, which took place during 2014, were a start in this direction as the meetings brought together people involved in data collection efforts from a number of countries and focused on how to move the agenda forward in a coordinate manner.

As noted in the section above, consensus is first needed on definitions to enable the building of an agreement on a common framework for data collection. A commitment of resources is then needed to invest in the necessary infrastructure to collect transaction level data. Trusted intermediaries will play a critical role in facilitating that data collection. The questions revolve around who should fund and also who should manage that data infrastructure. Finally, models and systems will be needed to analyse the data to provide the necessary evidence on what works.

It is however important to bear in mind that data collection should not become an end in itself and the purposes for data collection need to be *a priori* clear. The bulk of systematic evidence on SII will likely come from private data sources in earlier stages of market development. Fostering the collaboration between the different organisations collecting SII data through in surveys, polls and other approaches is important. While reaching a common understanding about definitions is vital, agreeing on a methodology to collect comparable cross-country data could provide the evidence base for a better understanding of the SII market. It can also help in the analysis of the role that policymaking can play in this area.

6.3.3. Primary impact measurement

SII targets the delivery of social outcomes at the same time as targeting financial returns (at least a return on capital): one without the other does not qualify as SII. Therefore the need for effective, robust and repeatable measurement of social outcomes is critical for social enterprises and investors. However developing effective, robust and repeatable measurement of social outcomes is easier said than done, and is certainly not as simple as calculating annual profits, especially when targets are part of the process (as in the case of SIBs). The social outcomes selected, measured and evaluated affect how attractive the enterprises is to financers, the business model used, how its practices encouraged or discouraged, internal decision-making, its level of cost effectiveness, and all together, the value of and regulation of SII practices as a whole. In short, getting it right is critical.

Particularly as global interest and activity in social impact investment is growing rapidly, better metrics for measuring at least primary (or "predetermined") social impact is needed. However, social benefits are difficult to value, measure and compare. In addition, the process of tracking and measuring these returns can be costly in terms time and resources.

The objectives behind measurement can differ for various stakeholders. Currently, SII measurement is focused on the achievements of the social delivery organisations. This information is helpful in evaluating the progress of the social ventures and can be useful in adjusting course as needed. However, it may not provide all of the necessary information investors are seeking regarding their future prospects (Rangan et al, 2013).

Investors need a set of tools for assessing social impact measurement. Further work will need to be done, likely by intermediaries, to strengthen investor understanding of the variety of impact metrics currently available (Jackson and Associates, 2012). The development of standard measurement systems will be an important step in further engaging mainstream investors (HM Government, 2013c). At the same time, it is critical to help social ventures, across different sectors, build greater capacity to measure social outcomes (Addis et al, 2013).

Currently many investors use proprietary measurement systems to determine social and environmental performance, if they are measuring impact in any systematic way at all (Rangan et al, 2011). Many investors rely on anecdotal evidence rather than real evidence (O'Donohoe et al., 2010). While a number of initiatives such as IRIS, SROI and CARS are working to develop standard measures and methodologies, further work in this area is needed (HM Government, 2013c). The European Commission has been working on this issue and one of the working groups of the international Social Impact Investment Taskforce has recently published a set of guidelines (WGIM, 2014), including an "impact value chain"(see Table 6.2 below).

The measurement of primary social impact is important for the market functioning (so demand and supply can more effectively communicate about return expectation and results) and has been the focus on impact measurement efforts to date. However, a better understanding of the broader or "secondary" social outcomes (spillover effects and positive externalities) and how social goods are delivered is also needed to fully determine the impact of social impact investment and assist policy decision making. As highlighted in Chapter 3, social outcomes can range from an individual to a society level. Also, the efficiency of interventions can either be at the individual level or more systemic. In addition, as discussed in Chapter 5, actions in one social area can have positive or negative spillovers in others and therefore need to be taken into account in a systemic approach. The next section addresses this broader approach.

Table 6.2. **WGIM guidelines for impact measurement**

	Guideline	Description
PLAN	Set goals	*Articulate the desired impact of the investments* Establish a clear investment thesis/Theory of Value Creation (ToVC) to form the basis of strategic planning and ongoing decision making and to serve as a reference point for investment performance
	Develop framework and elect metrics	*Determine metrics to be used for assessing the performance of the investments* Develop an effective impact measurement framework that integrates metrics and outlines how specific data are captured and used; utilise metrics that align with existing standards
DO	Collect and store data	*Capture and store data in a timely and organised fashion* Ensure that the information technology, tools, resources, human capital, and methods used to obtain and track data from investees function properly
	Validate data	*Validate data to ensure sufficient quality* Verify that impact data is complete and transparent by cross-checking calculations and assumptions against known data sources, where applicable
ASSESS	Analyse data	*Distil insights from the data collected* Review and analyse data to understand how investments are progressing against impact goals
REVIEW	Report data	*Share progress with key stakeholders* Distribute impact data coherently, credibly, and reliably to effectively inform decisions by all stakeholders
	Make data-driven investment management decisions	*Identify and implement mechanisms to strengthen the rigor of investment process and outcomes* Assess stakeholder feedback on reported data and address recommendations to make changes to the investment thesis or ToVC

Note: This table provides a summary of the impact measurement guidelines developed by the Working Group on Impact Measurement (WIGM). Please refer to "Impact Measurement: Guidelines for Good Impact Practice" for detailed guidelines and their application. Available at: https://iris.thegiin.org/guide/guidelines-for-good-impact-practice/summary.

Source: WGIM (2014).

6.4. Evaluation of broader social impact investment outcomes

The need for better evaluations of social impact investment outcomes for informing decisions in the area of SII, and its regulation, cannot be understated. What works can have long lasting effects on people's lives, and is part of the picture that determines the need for costly future social interventions. Yet, there are too few good quality evaluations suitable for informing market participants and policy makers about "what works", and most importantly "how" new policies and social innovations might be implemented.

While the context in each country is different and therefore the approaches will vary, we have outlined three key areas which might both make the market function more efficiently and help to evaluate the role of SII in meeting social needs, and thus the extent to which it should be supported through policy incentives. The first area is the development of relevant social outcome measures, that capture quality of life measures and their changes in both in the population (to identify need), and amongst recipients of the social intervention (to identify effectiveness). Second, contextual data, including general socio-economic conditions in households and communities and the levels and nature of general and specific social interventions, is required to develop appropriate controls for evaluation models. Third, robust and time-sensitive evaluations of policies, and/or aspects of policy innovation to more broadly inform implementation decisions, are needed (OECD, 2015b).

Some suggested steps to build this evidence base include:

- broader social outcomes of each intervention should be defined, including expected spill-over effects
- these social outcomes should be measurable independently of the policies' target measures, and include at least one distributional measure to retain a check on the "inclusivity" of the intervention effect.
- compulsory evaluations should be incorporated into the publicly funded interventions, publically incentivised forms of SII, or as part of formal regulation practices; and encouraged in independent forms of SII (this may require the development of a business case).
  - Evaluations need to be methodologically rigorous, and so support with the implementation of or methods for evaluations should be available as part of the development of a SII market, by sponsored independent researchers, or a formal regulatory body.
  - Timing of all social intervention evaluations should be predetermined and based on when social returns to interventions can be expected. More than one evaluation might be needed, as the same intervention may contribute to more than one outcome over time.
- Data techniques, such as data matching to administrative sources and national surveys, could be facilitated by governments and independent groups to provide access to contextual data in order to and improve the quality and efficiency of evaluation processes.

It is worth noting at this stage, that there is a trade-off between the need for timely policy interventions and the weight of - and wait for - the most rigorous evidence. Because it is important to act on social need in a timely way, there should be an expectation for "learning on the job". Risks associated with such an expectation can be limited first and foremost by piloting social interventions, by undertaking independent evaluations on untested aspects of the intervention, and preparing a recipient-focussed (pilot) "exit plan" with appropriate funding in place (OECD, 2015b).

6.4.1. Evaluating cost effectiveness or cost-benefit ratios?

Many governments may not have capacity and systems in place to measure cost-effectiveness of public service delivery, however, social impact investment can present a strategic opportunity for initiating the collection of such data. Clearly, these types of approaches would need to build over time with a balance being found between effective measurement and effective market development. Two types of evaluation methods are potentially relevant for assessing SII interventions: cost-benefit analysis (CBA) and cost-effectiveness analysis (CEA) (see OECD [2015b] for a more detailed discussion of these methods). Cost-benefit analysis (CBA) enables evaluators to compare the costs of a policy or intervention with its benefits measured in monetary terms (even if the benefits themselves are not pecuniary). Cost effectiveness analysis (CEA) compares the costs of meeting a given policy objective by alternative means.

The distinction is important. In the case of CBA, accurate information on the costs of meeting the objective must be available. Secondly, and most importantly, the program benefits must be *valued* even if they are not market goods (i.e. do not have a *price)*. By expressing costs and benefits in the same units, CBA is used to indicate whether a given policy objective is desirable When used on its' own CEA cannot help the policymaker decide what the policy objective should be since the benefits and costs are not expressed in the same units. This also means that it is impossible to compare across different policy domains. As such it cannot be used to determine whether the policy is welfare-improving in the strict sense. Rather CEA is used to determine the costs of meeting a given objective, and to compare between the costs of meeting that given objective through alternative means.

In the context of policy discussions related to SII the role of CBA is limited for a number of reasons. First, social impact investors and investees may have objectives related to social needs which are distinct from (and in many cases be more ambitious than) stated policy objectives. Second, the investor and the investee derive a value from the investment which may or nor may not be identical to that which is appropriate for the evaluation of public policy.[3]

The role of CEA in policy discussions about SII is more obvious. For instance, CEA can be applied to evaluate healthcare policies, for which it can be difficult to assess the monetary benefits but it is relatively straightforward to determine the desired outcome (e.g. "number of lives saved" or "DALYs" [EuropeAid, 2005]). CEA measures costs in monetary terms and compares them with the outcomes, expressed in terms of relevant units which related to the social need in question. The ratio of costs to effectiveness is computed in order to determine the cost per unit of effectiveness; the most effective projects will have lower cost-effectiveness ratios than alternatives.

This methodology is directly relevant for the case of SII. Firstly, investors and investees may well be interested in knowing whether or not their investments are meeting their objectives in terms of social needs at least cost. Secondly, policymakers would be interested in knowing whether different policy measures which incentivise the development of SII may be a more efficient way to meet their policy objective than more traditional state-managed forms of service delivery.

The evaluation should be as comprehensive as possible in the determination of costs and benefits, accounting for indirect and long-term effects of the program and reflecting the interests of all stakeholders involved (Better Evaluation, 2014a and 2014b). Interventions with social savings expectations and social outcomes expectation can undertake both forms of evaluations.

6.4.2. Measuring social impact: Selecting social outcome measures

Any type of social intervention is designed to achieve a social goal, SII is not different. The importance of measuring social outcomes was highlighted by the SIITF as well as by the Working Group on Impact Measurement (WGIM, 2014). The social outcomes defined by a social intervention should meet some standards, including: being predefined, measureable, valid, repeatable, and independent (not distortable). Social outcome monitoring may also include the addition of spillover measures, or time-sensitive changes to the social outcomes desired.

Predefined: Social impact investment should predefine its purpose, this allows for the intervention to be assessed on a common goal for all aspects of process and implementation. It allows other social impact investments to run complementary to it, and set expectations for social impact investors in the case of SII.

Measurable: Alone, whether an outcome is measurable is not enough to justify its selection, it also needs to accurately operationalise the predicted social outcome (see below). However, this is important because some aspects of a social intervention might be hard to measure (e.g. the preferences for care for dementia sufferers, or early year's children in childcare) and selecting unmeasurable outcomes will ultimately devalue future evaluations and bring into question the real impact. Whether monetised, (as may be required for SIBs), quality of life based (reduction in poverty) risk reducing (reduction in criminality) or efficiency enhancing (reductions in emergency service use) outcomes indicators should be – proxies or otherwise – the predefined outcome should be measureable.

Valid: A valid outcome measure accurately represents the desired outcomes, and is particularly important in the case of proxy measures for hard-to-measure outcomes. Inappropriate responses to social needs could occur if social enterprises focus their efforts on invalid representations of desired outcomes. Depending on the population being evaluated, and the type of outcomes being measures (particularly survey responses) outcomes measures may need to be validated during pilots to ensure they are not biased by gender, age or culture of the recipients – or generate biased non-response to evaluation requests.

Repeatable: In the case of multiple evaluations on the same measure, to determine outcomes or cost-effectiveness relative to a time frame, outcome measures need to be repeatable – insofar as they should be measured accurately more than once over a period of time (ensuring previous surveys or evaluations do not affect future measurement). For external validation of an intervention or its methods, or the transferability of an intervention, the measurement of the social outcome of interest should be repeatable in other settings.

Independent: Target setting may create incentives for selecting in easy-to-treat individuals into a social service, achieving measureable change but unequally. This can restrictive the inclusivity of social impact investment, and create further social problems down the line. Any outcome measure linked to payment-related targets should be measurable independently of the policies' target measures in order to assess "real change", and include at least one distributional measure to retain a check on the "inclusivity" of the intervention effect.

In some policy settings, an intervention may be expected to have spillover effects in other sectors, both positive and negative. Additional indicators may be needed to monitor these spillover effects for the purposes of addressing the "wrong pockets" problem (when returns to investment are found in other sectors), or adjusting a social impact score for SII based on negative externalities.

Finally, social impact investors and social delivery organisations should be prepared to adjust the outcome measures used to evaluate an intervention based on the time since the intervention occurred – these might be termed "accumulated outcomes" and valued accordingly. The Perry Preschool intervention, mentioned in Chapter 4, is a working example of this, where early years' interventions were still having positive social impacts decades later, but in the labour market and educational outcomes, as oppose to early years' outcomes of child health and parenting skills development. Equally, spillover outcomes may also be subject to this principal.

Box 6.1. **First Peterborough SIB outcome results**

On August 2014 the UK Ministry of Justice (MoJ) released the first results of the Peterborough SIB programme. This evaluation focuses on the outcome results of the SIB designed to meet pre-determined targets in terms of re-conviction rates.

The Government alongside the Big Lottery Fund (SIB commissioners) agreed to pay investors back their capital plus a return on their investment if there was an improvement of re-offending rates. These payments may reflect a proportion of the savings to the Government and wider benefits to the society that result from interventions by non-government delivery organisations and investors.

The measurement of the Peterborough SIB outcomes is designed around two cohorts of adult male offenders discharged from Peterborough prison. The first cohort includes individuals released between 9 September 2010 and 1 July 2012 after serving sentences of less than one year. The second cohort opened in July 2012.

The Peterborough SIB foresees that investors receive an outcome-based payment if one of the following scenarios materialises:

1. a reduction of 10% in the frequency of re-conviction events in each cohort of around 1 000 prisoners (from the baseline generated by a matched comparison group)
2. a reduction in re-conviction events of 7.5% or more detected across all 2 000 offenders in both cohorts, when measured against a matched comparison group.

The 10% and 7.5% thresholds were calculated, based on sample sizes and historical data, to ensure that any observed differences in re-offending rates between matched samples would be statistically significant. A statistically significant difference implies that outcomes payments are made for changes as a result of the SIB intervention and not due to unrelated factors.

The results of the first Peterborough cohort show a 8.4% reduction in terms of frequency of re-conviction events. This is below the required 10% reduction under condition 1) above, thus no payment is made to investors. However, the outcome result is above the 7.5% threshold under condition 2) above. Therefore, should the second cohort yield similar results, investors will be paid an agreed fixed sum per reduced re-conviction event.

Propensity Score Matching was used to calculate the percentage reduction in reoffending rates resulting from the Peterborough SIB approach. The cohort of 936 discharged offenders from Peterborough was matched against a national control group control group of 9 360 matched re-offenders discharged from other 34 male local prisons during the same period. The pre-matching samples included 31 207 observations from other prisons and 945 for Peterborough. The matching was done based 36 out of 38 demographic and criminal history variables such as offender age, ethnicity, nationality, number of past convictions or type of offence. The analysis was done based on detailed individual data provided by the MoJ and further information made available by Social Finance (the Peterborough SIB intermediary). Jolliffe and Hedderman (2014) provide further details on the data and methodological approach used.

Sources: MoJ (2014); Jolliffe and Hedderman (2014).

Another example is the recent evaluation of the first Social Impact Bond (SIB) that launched in 2010 as a new approach to address recidivism in the United Kingdom (see Chapter 2 for further background). The Peterborough SIB, developed and launched by Social Finance (SIB intermediary), provides pre- and post-release help to around 2 000 short-term prisoners aiming to reduce re-offending rates (by at least 7.5%) by the end of the pilot scheme. If the pilots are successful, outcome payments can reach USD 12.2 million from a total USD 7.6 investment. If social outcome thresholds are not met, investors will lose their cash. The initial results of the evaluation of the Peterborough SIB have recently been released and are described in Box 6.1.The preliminary results of the SIB model show that it has been successful thus far, both in terms of attracting funding to address social needs, as well as in effectively tackling social issues. However, there are a number of challenges and risks that should be taken into consideration when designing and implementing a SIB or other SII models including incentives and risks of unintended consequences, spillovers and cross-sector gains, and measurement risks.

In areas that involve complex and expensive social issues, no single SIB commissioner can justify making all of the outcomes payments. In the United Kingdom, the Social Outcomes Fund was created to address challenges related to spillovers and cross-sector gains – i.e. the returns on the provision of social services can accrue in distinct social areas. This fund leverages the contribution of outcomes-based commissions such as SIBs.

6.4.3. Methodologies and challenges for evaluating outcomes

Once an outcome, or set of outcomes, has been identified as a desirable result of social impact investment the next challenge for assessing impact of an SII-backed intervention is designing an appropriate evaluation.

Below is a checklist of questions to take into consideration:

- **What aspects to evaluate**: Clarify whether the intervention as a whole or aspects of the intervention are to be evaluated. Adjust or developing appropriate outcome indicators and controls accordingly.
- **Who to evaluate**: Recipients of the interventions, control groups, and extended populations (e.g. families of recidivists, communities, the general population) depending on the nature of the target population and expected spillovers.
- **When to evaluate**: Depending on the intervention (childcare vs. elderly care for instance), the expected outcome (e.g. long-term life outcomes for childcare, shorter periods for service take-up goals?), and should be timetabled in advance of the intervention (as part of the SII business plan).

- **How to evaluate**: consider piloting in the first instance, and identifying suitable control groups for control trials (for details of this method see chapter 3 of OECD, 2015a), in absence of this tailored survey data pre, during and post interventions, or pre-existing surveys might allow for difference-in-difference tests. For expectation of long-term returns, longitudinal cohort data may be useful. Cost benefit analysis should be included as standard, as should contextual description of governance and implementation practice for the purposes of transferability

Notes

1. http://iipcollaborative.org/london-principles/.

2. For further details on these policy actions see: www.socialimpactinvestment.org/.

3. For example in the case of CBA it is important to draw a distinction between paternalistic and non-paternalistic altruism, and it is only the former which is relevant when ascertaining whether or not a policy intervention is welfare-improving. See Johansson (1992) for a discussion.

References

Addis, R., J. McLeod, and A. Raine (2013), "IMPACT Australia: Investment for Social and Economic Benefit", Australian Government, Department of Education, Employment and Workplace Relations, November.

Better Evaluation (2014a) "Cost Benefit Analysis". Accessed at the Better Evaluation website 16 April 2014, www.betterevaluation.org.

Better Evaluation (2014b) "Cost Effectiveness Analysis". Accessed at the Better Evaluation website 16 April 2014 www.betterevaluation.org.

O'Donohoe, N., C. Leijonhufvud and Y. Saltuk (2010), "Impact Investments: An Emerging Asset Class", J.P. Morgan Securities plc, GIIN and Rockefeller Foundation, November.

EuropeAid (2005) "Cost Effectiveness analysis". Accessed at the EuropeAid website 16 April 2014 http://ec.europa.eu/europeaid/index_en.htm.

HM Government, United Kingdom (2013c), "G8 Social Impact Investment Forum: Outputs and Agreed Actions", UK Cabinet Office, London, July.

HM Government, United Kingdom (2011), "Growing the Social Investment Market: A vision and strategy", UK Cabinet Office, London, February.

IIPC (2014), "Impact Investing Policy in 2014: A snapshot of global activity", Impact Investing Policy Collaborative, November.

Jackson, E.T. & Associates (2012), "Accelerating Impact: Achievements, Challenges and What's Next in the Impact Investing Industry", The Rockefeller Foundation, July.

Johansson, P. (1992), "Altruism in Cost-Benefit Analysis" in *Environmental and Resource Economics*, 6(2): 605-13.

Jolliffe, D. and C. Hedderman (2014) "Peterborough Social Impact Bond: Final Report on Cohort 1 Analysis". Available at: https://www.gov.uk/government/uploads/system/uploads/attachment_data/file/341684/peterborough-social-impact-bond-report.pdf.

MoJ (2014) "Peterborough Social Impact Bond; HMP Doncaster; Payment by Results pilots: Final re-conviction results for cohorts 1" *Statistics Bulletin*, Ministry of Justice, London, August.

NAB-AUS (2014), "Delivering on Impact", National Advisory Board Report, Australia, Social Impact Investment Taskforce established by the G8, September.

NAB-CAN (2014), "Mobilizing Private Capital for Public Good: Priorities for Canada", National Advisory Board Report, Canada, Social Impact Investment Taskforce established by the G8, September.

NAB-GER (2014), "Wirkungsorientiertes Investierenn: Neue Finanzierungsquellen zur Lösung gesellschaftlicher Herausforderungen", National Advisory Board Report, Germany, Social Impact Investment Taskforce established by the G8, September.

NAB-FRA (2014), "Comment et pourquoi favoriser des investissements à impact social ? Innover financièrement pour innover socialement", National Advisory Board Report, France, Social Impact Investment Taskforce established by the G8, September.

NAB-ITA (2014), "La finanza che include: gli investimenti ad impatto sociale per una nuova economia", National Advisory Board Report, Italy, Social Impact Investment Taskforce established by the G8, September.

NAB-JAP (2014), "The Social Impact Investment Landscape in Japan", National Advisory Board Report, Japan, Social Impact Investment Taskforce established by the G8, September.

NAB-UK (2014), "Building a social impact investment market: The UK experience", National Advisory Board Report, United Kingdom, Social Impact Investment Taskforce established by the G8, September.

NAB-US (2014), "Private Capital Public Good: How Smart Federal Policy Can Galvanize Impact Investing — and Why It's Urgent", National Advisory Board Report, United States, Social Impact Investment Taskforce established by the G8, June.

OECD (2015a), "Comparing the effectiveness and efficiency of family cash benefits and services" internal working document, Directorate for Employment, Labour and Social Affairs.

OECD (2015b), Integrated Service Delivery for Vulnerable Groups.

Rangan, K.V., S. Appleby, and L. Moon (2011), "The Promise of Impact Investing", Harvard Business School, Background Note No. 512-045, Boston.

Thornley, B., D. Wood, K. Grace and S. Sullivant (2011), "Impact Investing: A Framework for Policy Design and Analysis", Pacific Community Ventures, Institute for Responsible Investment at Harvard University, and Rockefeller Foundation, January.

WEF (2012), "Breaking the Binary: A Policy Guide to Scaling Social Innovation", World Economic Forum, New York.

WGIM (2014), "Impact Measurement: Shifting the Paradigm", Working Group on Impact Measurement (WGIM), Social Impact Investment Taskforce established by the G8, September.

Annex 6.1

Examples of policy instruments in G7 countries and Australia

Country	Name	Type	Link
AUS	Social Enterprise Development and Investment Funds (SEDIF)	Supply	http://employment.gov.au/social-enterprise-development-and-investment-funds
CAN	RISQ Fund (Quebec)	Supply	www.fonds-risq.qc.ca/
CAN	Fiducie du Chantier de l'économie sociale (Quebec)	Supply	http://fiducieduchantier.qc.ca/?lang=eng
CAN	SVX trading platform (Ontario)	Intermediaries	www.svx.ca/
CAN	Social Enterprise Demonstration Fund (Ontario)	Supply	https://www.ontario.ca/business-and-economy/social-enterprise-demonstration-fund
CAN	Toronto's Centre for Social Innovation	Demand	http://socialinnovation.ca/
CAN	Community Contribution Companies (C3, British Columbia)	Tax and regulation	www.fin.gov.bc.ca/prs/ccc/
CAN	Community Interest Companies (CIC , Nova Scotia)	Tax and regulation	http://nslegislature.ca/legc/bills/61st_4th/1st_read/b153.htm
CAN	Social Innovation Fund (Alberta)	Supply	http://humanservices.alberta.ca/social-innovation-fund.html
CAN	Immigrant Access Fund	Supply	www.iafcanada.org/
Europe	EUSEF	Tax and regulation	See Box 3.5
Europe	Social impact accelerator	Supply	www.eif.org/what_we_do/equity/sia/index.htm
FRA	LOI n° 2014-856 : Économie Sociale et Solidaire	Tax and regulation	www.legifrance.gouv.fr/affichTexte.do?cidTexte=JORFTEXT000029313296&categorieLien=id
FRA	BPI France planning to provide funding	Supply	www.bpifrance.fr/Vivez-Bpifrance/Actualites/Economie-sociale-et-solidaire-decouvrez-le-rapport-d-etape-de-Bpifrance-sur-le-financement-de-l-ESS
ITA	Legge delega di riforma del Terzo Settore	Tax and regulation	www.governo.it/Governo/ConsiglioMinistri/dettaglio.asp?d=76205

Country	Name	Type	Link
ITA	Specific social cooperatives legislation	Tax and regulation	(in certain regions only)
ITA	Bank foundation legislation	Tax and regulation	
ITA	Normativa sul Microcredito	Tax and regulation	http://microcreditoitalia.org/index.php?option=com_content&view=article&id=335&Itemid=353&lang=it
ITA	L'Ente Nazionale per il Microcredito	Other	http://microcreditoitalia.org/index.php?lang=it
ITA	Titoli di Solidarietà (D.Lgs n. 460/1997)	Tax and regulation	www.normattiva.it/uri-res/N2Ls?urn:nir:stato:decreto.legislativo:1997;460
JAP	Legal amendment to the corporate law	Tax and regulation	
JAP	New Public Commons	Other	www5.cao.go.jp/npc/index-e/index-e.html
JAP	Social Innovation Forum	Demand	http://japan-social-innovation-forum.net/
JAP	Osaka Prefectural Government's Social Entrepreneur Support Project	Supply	www.pref.osaka.lg.jp/chiikifukushi/kigyouka/syakaikigyoukafand.html
UK	Community Investment Tax Relief	Tax and regulation	www.hmrc.gov.uk/specialist/citc_guidance.htm
UK	Futurebuilders	Supply	www.futurebuilders-england.org.uk/
UK	Community Interest Company (CIC)	Tax and regulation	https://www.gov.uk/government/organisations/office-of-the-regulator-of-community-interest-companies
UK	Dormant Bank and Building Society Account Act	Tax and regulation	https://www.gov.uk/government/publications/review-of-the-dormant-bank-and-building-society-accounts-act-2008
UK	Investment and Contract Readiness Fund (ICRF)	Demand	www.beinvestmentready.org.uk/about/
UK	Big Society Capital (BSC)	Intermediaries	www.bigsocietycapital.com/
UK	Social Outcomes Fund	Supply	http://blogs.cabinetoffice.gov.uk/socialimpactbonds/outcomes-fund/
UK	Commissioning Academy	Supply	https://www.gov.uk/the-commissioning-academy-information
UK	Social Value Act	Other	https://www.gov.uk/government/publications/public-services-social-value-act-2012-1-year-on
UK	Unit Cost Database	Other	http://data.gov.uk/sib_knowledge_box/toolkit
UK	Social Investment Tax Relief (SITR)	Tax and regulation	www.hmrc.gov.uk/sitr/
US	Small Business Investment Company Impact Investment Fund	Supply	www.sba.gov/category/lender-navigation/sba-loan-programs/sbic-program/general-information/impact-investment-sbic

Country	Name	Type	Link
US	Program-Related Investments	Tax and regulation	www.irs.gov/Charities-&-Non-Profits/Private-Foundations/Program-Related-Investments
US	Community Reinvestment Act	Other	www.federalreserve.gov/communitydev/cra_about.htm
US	Low-Income Housing Tax Credit	Tax and regulation	http://portal.hud.gov/hudportal/HUD?src=/program_offices/comm_planning/affordablehousing/training/web/lihtc/basics
US	National Housing Trust Fund	Supply	http://nlihc.org/issues/nhtf
US	Riegle Community Development and Regulatory Improvement Act	Tax and regulation	https://www.govtrack.us/congress/bills/103/hr3474
US	Community Development Financial Institutions Fund	Supply/ demand	www.cdfifund.gov/
US	New Markets Tax Credit	Tax and regulation	www.irs.gov/pub/irs-utl/atgnmtc.pdf

Note: Information on Germany is available (NAB_GER, 2014) but not yet in English and will be added once available. SIBs are considered as policy instruments but are not included in this table because they are exhaustively covered in Annex 2.1, Chapter 2. This table excludes policy instruments targeting areas or activity that does not fit within the OECD working definition presented in Chapter 4. The table only provides information on SII-specific policy instruments. Therefore, policy instruments that affect SII but do not necessarily target the SII ecosystem (e.g. seed funds; regulations on institutional investors asset allocation and risk) are excluded.

Source: OECD, based on National Advisory Board (NAB) reports: NAB_AUS (2014), NAB_CAN (2014), NAB_GER (2014), NAB_FRA (2014), NAB_ITA (2014), NAB_JAP (2014), NAB_UK (2014), NAB_US (2014).

Glossary

Angel investors

An angel investor is an individual investor (qualified as defined by some national regulations) that invests directly (or through their personal holding) their own money predominantly in seed or start-up companies with no family relationships. Angel investors make their own (final) investment decisions and are financially independent, *i.e.* a possible total loss of their investments will not significantly change the economic situation of their assets. Angel investors invest with a medium to long term set time-frame and are ready to provide, on top of their individual investment, follow-up strategic support to entrepreneurs from investment to exit. (OECD, 2012)

Asset Lock

The Asset Lock is a restriction on the transfer of assets. Asset Lock is designed to ensure that the assets of companies (including any profits or other surpluses generated by its activities) are used for the benefit of the community. (Adapted from BIS, 2013.)

Catalytic (first-loss) capital

Catalytic (first-loss) capital (CFLC) entails a capital provider that will bear first losses (the amount of loss covered is typically set and agreed upon upfront). By improving the recipient's risk-return profile, CFLC catalyses the participation of investors that otherwise would not have participated. CFLC aims to channel commercial capital towards the achievement of certain social and/or environmental outcomes. In addition, the purpose can also be to demonstrate the commercial viability of investing into a new market. CFLC is a tool that can be incorporated into a capital structure via a range of financial instruments (authors based on GIIN, 2013).

Community investing

Community investing refers to the provision of financial services to underserved communities and includes banks, credit unions, loan funds, and venture capital funds. (Freireich and Fulton 2009)

Corporate social responsibility (CSR)

CSR is defined as the integration of business operations and values, where the interests of all stakeholders – including investors, customers, employees, the community, and the environment – are reflected in the company's policies and actions. Special attention is given to corporate practices as they relate to environmental, social, and governance (ESG) performance. (Source: Adapted from Freireich and Fulton, 2009)

Cost-benefit analysis (CBA)

Cost-benefit analysis is a technique used to compare the total costs of a programme/project with its benefits, using a common metric (most commonly monetary units). This enables the calculation of the net cost or benefit associated with the programme. (Better Evaluation, 2014a)

Cost-efficiency analysis (CEA)

Cost-effectiveness analysis is an alternative to cost-benefit analysis (CBA). The technique compares the relative costs to the outcomes (effects) of two or more courses of action. (Better Evaluation, 2014b)

Impact investing

Impact investments are investments made into companies, organisations, and funds with the intention to generate social and environmental impact alongside a financial return. Impact investments can be made in both emerging and developed markets, and target a range of returns from below market to market rate, depending upon the circumstances. The practice of impact investing is further defined by the following four core characteristics: i) intentionality; ii) investment with return expectations; iii) range of return expectations and asset classes; and iv) impact measurement. (Source: GIIN website)

Market failure

Market failure is a general term describing situations in which market outcomes are not Pareto efficient. Market failures provide a rationale for government intervention. (OECD Glossary of Statistical Terms)

Mission-driven investing (MRI)

MRI is a term used to describe mission-related investments that are market-rate investments of endowment funds that align with the social or environmental mission of a foundation. MRI can include the use of social investing tools and sometimes including shareholder advocacy and positive and negative screening. (Source: Rangan et al., 2011)

Non-profit institutions (NPI)

Non-profit institutions are legal or social entities created for the purpose of producing goods and services whose status does not permit them to be a source of income, profit, or other financial gain for the units that establish, control or finance them. In practice their productive activities are bound to generate either surpluses or deficits but any surpluses they happen to make cannot be appropriated by other institutional units. (UN, 1993)

Program related investments (PRIs)

Investments, which often take the form of loans, loan guarantees, or equity investments that are derived from a foundation's assets but count toward its charitable distribution requirement. Generally, these investments yield below-market-rate returns for the foundation. (Source: INSEAD based on Lawrence and Mukai, 2011)

Sample size

The number of sampling units which are to be included in the sample. In the case of a multi-stage sample this number refers to the number of units at the final stage in the sampling. (OECD Glossary of Statistical Terms)

Sample survey

A sample survey is a survey which is carried out using a sampling method, i.e. in which a portion only, and not the whole population is surveyed. (OECD Glossary of Statistical Terms)

Services, social

Social (and collective) services provide final consumption for households and are distinctive for their non-market character in most OECD countries. Collective consumption decisions and public financing are common, as is production by governments, non-profit organisations and subsidised private organisations. Social services comprise the following International Standard Industrial Classification (ISIC) Rev. 3 sub-groups:

- government proper (civil or military)
- health services
- educational services
- miscellaneous social services.

(OECD Glossary of Statistical Terms)

Social benefits

Social benefits are current transfers received by households intended to provide for the needs that arise from certain events or circumstances, for example, sickness, unemployment, retirement, housing, education or family circumstances. (OECD Glossary of Statistical Terms)

Social business

A non-loss, non-dividend company designed to address a societal problem through a market-based business model. It is distinct from a non-profit because the business should seek to generate a modest profit which will be used to expand the company's reach, improve the product or service or in other ways subsidise the social mission. (Source: INSEAD adapted from Yunus, 2009).

Social context

Social context refers to variables that, while not usually the direct target of policy, are crucial for understanding the context within which social policy is developed. (OECD Glossary of Statistical Terms)

Social enterprise

Any private activity conducted in the public interest, organised with an entrepreneurial strategy but whose main purpose is not the maximisation of profit but the attainment of certain economic and social goals, and which has a capacity of bringing innovative solutions to the problems of social exclusion and unemployment. (Source: OECD, 2000)

Social expenditure

Social expenditure is the provision by public (and private) institutions of benefits to, and financial contributions targeted at, households and individuals in order to provide support during circumstances which adversely affect their welfare, provided that the provision of the benefits and financial contributions constitutes neither a direct payment for a particular good or service nor an individual contract or transfer. Such benefits can be cash transfers, or can be the direct ("in-kind") provision of goods and services. (OECD Glossary of Statistical Terms)

Social impact bond (SIB)

A Social Impact Bond is a financial mechanism in which investors pay for a set of interventions to improve a social outcome that is of social and/or financial interest to a government commissioner. If the social outcome improves, the government commissioner repays the investors for their initial investment plus a return for the financial risks they took. If the social outcomes are not achieved, the investors stand to lose their investment. (Social Finance website)[1]

Social impact investment (SII)

Investments made into businesses and social sector organisations, directly or through funds, with the intention of generating a measurable, beneficial social and environmental impact alongside a financial return. (SIITF, 2014a)

Social Impact Investment is a transaction between an investor and investee in a social area, targeting beneficiaries in need. Beneficiaries targeted should be at risk populations and the good provided should have a mix of public and private good characteristics. These transactions are often made using intermediaries. The investee in the transaction should, at least, inscribe a compulsory reporting clause of its social activity in the statutes, as well as provide a formal evaluation of social impact. In parallel, the investor should, at least, have a compulsory reporting clause for social impact investments and have return expectations above or equal to zero, but not above the market rate of return (actual return may be higher). (OECD working definition, 2014)

Social investment

Social investment is the provision and use of capital with the aim of generating social as well as financial returns. Social investment carries an expectation of repayment of some or all of the finance. It can cover loans, equity, bonds, and is sometimes used alongside other instruments, such as guarantees or underwriting. As with any other investments, where the investee business performs well, returns generated may be principally reinvested in the business, as well as offered to investors. Investors in social outcomes weigh up the balance between the social and financial returns which they expect from an investment, according to their own priorities. They will often accept lower financial returns in order to generate greater social impact. (Source: City of London, 2012)

Social purpose organisation (SPO)

An SPO, whether nonprofit, for-profit, or hybrid, seeks to create positive social impact for human society, animals, or the natural environment in the form of social value that is not limited to economic wealth for owners or consumption benefits for customers. (Source: Clark et al., 2012).

Socially responsible investing (SRI)

SRI is an investment approach that generally employs negative screening to avoid investing in harmful companies which are creating negative spillovers in society through their activities (e.g. Tobacco companies, weapon manufacturers). Today large amounts are invested under an SRI approach which has implications for shareholder activism/advocacy to be able to encourage corporate social responsibility practices. (Source: INSEAD adapted from Palandjian, 2010)

Target population

The set of elements about which information is wanted and estimates are required. Practical considerations may dictate that some units are excluded (e.g., institutionalised individuals, the homeless, or those that are not possible to access without incurring excessive cost). (OECD Glossary of Statistical Terms)

Venture philanthropy

Venture Philanthropy is an approach to build stronger investee organisations with a societal purpose by providing them with both financial and nonfinancial support in order to increase their societal impact. The venture philanthropy approach includes the use of the entire spectrum of financing instruments (grants, equity, debt, etc.) and pays particular attention to the ultimate objective of achieving societal impact. The approach includes both social investment and high engagement grant making. (Source: EVPA website).

Note

1. Available at: www.socialfinance.org.uk/services/social-impact-bonds/.

References

BIS (2013) "Office of the Regulator of Community Interest Companies: information and guidance notes", Department for Businesses, Innovation and Skills, London, March.

City of London (2012), "A Brief Handbook on Social Investment", City of London Corporation, London, February. Source: GIIN website

Clark, C., J. Emerson, and B. Thornley (2012), "A Market Emerges: The Six Dynamics of Impact Investing", Pacific Community Ventures, ImpactAssets and CASE at Duke University's Fuqua School of Business, October.

GIIN (2013), "Catalytic First-loss Capital", New York, October.

INSEAD (nd), "Glossary of Terms for Social Entrepreneurship and Impact Investing", www.globalimpactforum.com/program/insead/glossary/index (accessed 11 September 2013).

OECD (2000), *Social Enterprises*, OECD Publishing, http://dx.doi.org/10.1787/9789264182332-en.

OECD (2008), *OECD Glossary of Statistical Terms*, OECD Publishing, http://dx.doi.org/10.1787/9789264055087-en.

OECD (2012), "Preliminary Results of the OECD Seed and Early Stage Financing Questionnaire", internal working document, Directorate for Science, Technology and Industry.

Palandjian, T. (2010), "Investing for Impact: Case Studies across Asset Classes", Bridges Ventures, Parthenon Group and GIIN, London, January.

UN (1993), *System of National Accounts*, United Nations, New York.

Yunus, M. (2009), "Creating a World Without Poverty: Social Business and the Future of Capitalism", *PublicAffairs*.

Annex A. OECD Expert meetings: List of participants

Paris, 21 March 2014 and London, 18 June 2014

Ms. Rosemary ADDIS	Executive Director Impact Strategist Co-founder, Impact Investing	Australia
Mr. Jake BENFORD	Senior Project Manager Bertelsmann Foundation	Germany
Ms Sandy BLACKBURN-WRIGHT	Executive Director Impact Strategist Co-founder, Impact Investing Australia	Australia
Mr. Amit BOURI	Managing Director Global Impact Investing Network	United States
Mr. Kieron BOYLE	Head of Social Investment and Finance UK Cabinet Office	United Kingdom
Dr. Stephen BRIEN	Chair's Executive Team Social Impact Investment Taskforce	United Kingdom
Mr. Adrian BROWN	Principal Boston Consulting Group	United Kingdom
Professor Mario CALDERINI	Department of Management, Economics and Industrial Engineering Politecnico di Milano	Italy
Ms. Radana CRHOVA	Senior Economist Office for Civil Society, Government Innovation Group UK Cabinet Office	United Kingdom
Ms. Aimie COLE	Chair's Executive Team Social Impact Investment Taskforce	United Kingdom
Ms. Carolien DE BRUIN	Specialist Leader Monitor Institute	United States
Mr. François DE WITT	President FINANSOL	France
Ms. Sarah DOYLE	Senior Policy Advisor MaRS Centre for Impact Investing	Canada
Mr. Guilhem DUPUY	Attaché de Direction Générale ECOFI Investissements	France
Dr. Danilo Giovanni FESTA	General Director Ministry of Labour and Social Policy	Italy

Ms. Stephanie GIAMPORCARO	Senior Lecturer Bertha Centre for Social Innovation and Entrepreneurship, Graduate School of Business, University of Cape Town	South Africa
Mr. Gunnar GLÄNZEL	Senior Researcher Centre for Social Investment, Heidelberg University	Germany
Ms. Paula GOLDMAN	Senior Director, Knowledge & Advocacy Omidyar Network	United States
Dr. Riccardo GRAZIANO	Director General National Microcredit Agency	Italy
Dr. Siobhan HARTY	Director General, Social Policy Employment and Social Development Canada	Canada
Dr. Lisa HEHENBERGER	Research Director European Venture Philanthropy Association	EU
Ms. Diana HOLLMANN	Deutsche Gesellschaft für Internationale Zusammenarbeit (GIZ) GmbH	Germany
Mr. Richard JOHNSON	Chairman, BIAC Technology Committee CEO Global Helix LLC	United States
Mr. Nigel KERSHAW	CEO Chairman, The Big Issue Ltd Big Issue Invest	United Kingdom
Professor Mario LA TORRE	Professor of Banking and Finance Department of Management - Banking and Finance University of Rome " La Sapienza"	Italy
Ms. Alexandra MEAGHER	Policy Advisor Social Investment and Finance team UK Cabinet Office	United Kingdom
Ms. Jane NEWMAN	International Director Social Finance UK	United Kingdom
Professor Alex NICHOLLS	Professor of Social Entrepreneurship Said Business School, Oxford University	United Kingdom
Mr. Nick O'DONOHOE	Chief Executive Officer Big Society Capital	United Kingdom
Ms. Stephanie PETRICK	Director Social Investment Impact in Motion	Germany
Mr. Karl RICHTER	CEO and Co-founder Engaged Investment - EngagedX	United Kingdom
Mr. Matt ROBINSON	Director of Strategy & Market Development Big Society Capital	United Kingdom
Ms. Yasemin SALTUK	Executive Director of Research J P Morgan	United Kingdom
M. Hugues SIBILLE	Vice-Président Présidence, Groupe Crédit Coopératif	France

Ms. Julie SUNDERLAND	PRI Program Director Bill & Melinda Gates Foundation	United States
Ms. Louise SWISTEK	Investment Manager Le Comptoir de l'Innovation	France
Dr. Volker THEN	Managing Director Centre for Social Investment University of Heidelberg	Germany
Ms. Marilou VAN GOLSTEIN BROUWERS	Managing Director Triodos Investment Management BV	Netherlands
Mme Nadia VOISIN	Conseillère soutien au secteur privé dans les pays en développement Direction Générale de la Mondialisation et des Partenariats Ministère des Affaires Etrangères Sous-Direction de la Sécurité Alimentaire et du Développement humain	France
Mr. Arthur WOOD	Founding Partner Total Impact Advisors	Switzerland

ORGANISATION FOR ECONOMIC CO-OPERATION AND DEVELOPMENT

The OECD is a unique forum where governments work together to address the economic, social and environmental challenges of globalisation. The OECD is also at the forefront of efforts to understand and to help governments respond to new developments and concerns, such as corporate governance, the information economy and the challenges of an ageing population. The Organisation provides a setting where governments can compare policy experiences, seek answers to common problems, identify good practice and work to co-ordinate domestic and international policies.

The OECD member countries are: Australia, Austria, Belgium, Canada, Chile, the Czech Republic, Denmark, Estonia, Finland, France, Germany, Greece, Hungary, Iceland, Ireland, Israel, Italy, Japan, Korea, Luxembourg, Mexico, the Netherlands, New Zealand, Norway, Poland, Portugal, the Slovak Republic, Slovenia, Spain, Sweden, Switzerland, Turkey, the United Kingdom and the United States. The European Union takes part in the work of the OECD.

OECD Publishing disseminates widely the results of the Organisation's statistics gathering and research on economic, social and environmental issues, as well as the conventions, guidelines and standards agreed by its members.

OECD PUBLISHING, 2, rue André-Pascal, 75775 PARIS CEDEX 16
(93 2015 01 1 P) ISBN 978-92-64-22893-1 – 2015